BERKELEY

Bruce Umbaugh
Webster University

 **Wadsworth**
Thomson Learning.™

Australia • Canada • Mexico • Singapore • Spain
United Kingdom • United States

To Martha

Printed in the United States of America
1 2 3 4 5 6 7 03 02 01 00 99

For permission to use material from this text, contact us:
Web: www.thomsonrights.com
Fax: 1-800-730-2215
Phone: 1-800-730-2214

For more information, contact:
Wadsworth/Thomson Learning
10 Davis Drive
Belmont, CA 94002-3098
USA
http://www.wadsworth.com

ISBN: 0-534-57619-2

Table of Contents

Preface vi

Note on References vii

Introduction 1
    To Be Is To Be Perceived 1
    Berkeley's Life 4
    Intellectual Context 9

Why Matter Does Not Exist 18
    Berkeley's warning 18
    Language and meaning 19
    Against the existence of matter 22

Objections and Replies 33
    If a tree falls in the forest 33
    Unperceived Objects 34
    Science 38
    Is Berkeley a Subjectivist? 42

God 48
    God's Role 48
    Berkeley's Three Arguments for God ... 49

Problems 55
    Objects 55
    Minds 60

Responses 64
    Empiricism at Its Limits 64
    After Kant 71
    The 20th Century and Beyond 74

Notes 82

Bibliography 86

Preface

Berkeley was my first philosophical love. As a high school student, I was amazed by his theories and astounded further by the clarity of his arguments. I thought to myself, "Can you believe it?!" and "How can you not?!" My adolescent delight in the shock value of philosophy gave way over time to a richer appreciation the more I studied Berkeley's thought. As the last section of this work shows, his ideas inform my thinking about even the most contemporary metaphysical and epistemological subjects.

It is a commonplace that books do not happen on their own. Dan Kolak displayed both patience and philosophical acumen in editing this book. In addition to my debt to him, I owe intellectual debts to many of my teachers, at all levels, both those who taught me about Berkeley and those who otherwise inspired. I hope that this small book is at least some token repayment, and I offer also some further resources available at http://www.webster.edu/philosophy/OnBerkeley/ (no period). I am grateful, too, for the insights and advice provided by anonymous reviewers.

Mel and Miles robbed me of sleep, but they repay me in laughter.

Finally, as much as I owe the others, as much as I first loved Berkeley, and so very much more: to Martha.

Note on References

References to Berkeley's works appear in the main text. References to other works and discussion will be confined to end notes.

Quotations draw mainly from the IntelLex Past Masters editions of Berkeley's works. To facilitate reading quotations in context, a generic system of reference is adopted here. This should permit interested readers to find referenced passages in any standard edition of the work in question. References are made:

by entry number for the *Commonplace Books* (or *Philosophical Commentaries*) [C #];

by section number for *An Essay Towards a new Theory of Vision* [V #];

by section number for the "Introduction" of *A Treatise Concerning the Principles of Human Knowledge* [I #];

by section number for Part One of *A Treatise Concerning the Principles of Human Knowledge* (or, *Principles*) [P #];

by Dialogue number and paragraph for *Three Dialogues Between Hylas and Philonous* (or *Dialogues*) [D #:##];

by section number for *De Motu* [M #];

by Dialogue number and paragraph for *Alciphron, or, a minute philosopher* (or *Alciphron*) [A #:##].

1
Introduction

To Be Is To Be Perceived

Just as René Descartes' philosophy is identified with the famous phrase, "*cogito, ergo sum*" ("I think, therefore I am"), George Berkeley's is linked to "*esse* is *percipi*" ("to be is to be perceived"). Descartes and Berkeley both accord the thinking and perceiving mind a central philosophical role. Berkeley, though, thinks that the concept of "matter" is illicit; material substance does not exist. Instead, real things are ideas in minds. In spite–or because–of that fact, Berkeley says, we have scientific knowledge of the real world.

Berkeley is an *empiricist:* he rejects whatever cannot be justified by experience or reason. The things we experience exist; in this Berkeley agrees with ordinary people everywhere. But Berkeley also agrees with the learned philosophers and scientists who maintain that what people experience immediately is something in their minds or consciousness. So, Berkeley puts the two together in holding that, for "unthinking things," *esse* is *percipi:* their being consists in their being perceived. All his lines of reasoning should be understood in the light of that claim, whether arguing for it, interpreting it, or defending it against objections.

Berkeley begins by agreeing with philosophers such as Descartes and John Locke that what we immediately sense are our own ideas. By "ideas," they do not mean "flashes of insight," or "opinions," but something including thoughts and mental images. They saw that I and my perceptions of things seem to form the central point from which I might hope to establish truths about the world. My perceptions obviously depend somehow on me; the very idea of my thoughts or emotions existing without me–that is either independent of me or outside me–is bizarre:

> That neither our thoughts, nor passions, nor ideas formed by the imagination exist without the mind is what everybody will allow.

But Berkeley continues:

> And (to me) it seems no less evident that the various sensations or ideas imprinted on the sense, however blended or combined together (that is whatever objects they compose), cannot exist otherwise than in a mind perceiving them. [P 3]

Our thoughts and imaginings exist in our minds, and we sense our sensations, and perceive our perceptions. Moreover, Berkeley contends that *objects* are also made of ideas or sensations and, so, require the perceiver's mind just as much. Why does he think that? Well, how do we know real things exist? Only because we experience them. He continues:

> I think an intuitive knowledge may be obtained of this by anyone who shall attend to what is meant by the term *exist* when applied to sensible things. The table I write on, I say, exists; that is, I see and feel it; and if I were out of my study, I should say that it existed–meaning by that that if I was in my study I might perceive it or that some other spirit actually does perceive it.

We know the existence of real things, Berkeley says, by sensing them. Moreover, what we *mean* by "the table in my office exists" is "I perceive it, or would if I were in the office properly situated, or someone else is perceiving it." But I can only make sense of claims about the table in terms of experience. Whatever the "reality of my table" is, my seeing and hearing *it* is taken to be mediated by a collection of sensations or perceptions: sights, sounds, touches, smells, and tastes.

There was an odor; that is, it was smelled; there was a sound, that is to say, it was heard; a color or figure, and it was perceived by sight or touch. This is all that I can understand by these and the like expressions. For as to what is said of the absolute existence of unthinking things without any relation to their being perceived that seems perfectly unintelligible. Their *esse* is *percipi,* nor is it possible they should have any existence out of the minds or thinking things which perceive them. [P 3]

I, a "thinking thing," experience a collection of perceptions that I call "my table." [P 1] If I were to be drugged or dreaming or hit in the eye, I might "sense" two tables beside me, at least in one meaning of "sense." In reality, there would still only be the one table. If I am limited to evidence of myself and my sensations it appears difficult to establish anything else about the world. Descartes confronted this "ego-centric predicament." When he centered his system of thought on the existence of his own self—his "ego"—the raw materials for making sense of the world did not include anything outside him. This predicament drives much philosophizing about knowledge in the early modern period.

Berkeley departs from many of these other thinkers, though, in his philosophical aspirations and intentions. Where both Descartes and Locke were focused on trying to set forth philosophical foundations adequate to the new science being advanced by Galileo or Newton, Berkeley is more concerned to reconcile what he took to be the common sense view of things with the emerging scientific world picture. To do so, he had to show that science made sense within the framework that he developed.

In trying to develop such a system, Berkeley derives an apparently outlandish theory—the one about real things being ideas--from modest conclusions that anyone of his contemporaries—or readers of this book for that matter—would accept. Perhaps for its apparent counter-intuitiveness, Berkeley is among the most misunderstood of the acknowledged "greats" in Western philosophy.

Many other philosophers and scientists in the 17th and 18th centuries held that the "real stuff" of the universe comprised particles much, much too small for us to see. These tiny particles cause all of our experiences, they said: hearing a dog bark, tasting cappuccino ice cream, smelling diesel exhaust, feeling a snowflake melt, or seeing the Perseids.

Berkeley argues against this position, and, so, against every major scientist of his day. Berkeley holds that *there is no such thing as matter or material substance.* There are no other objects hiding behind the immediate objects of perception, holding them up for our inspection. There are, Berkeley says, no particles too small for us to see but constituting what is "really real" in the universe. Instead, there are thinking things, and there are unthinking things. Unthinking things are ideas. To be more exact, since ideas cannot subsist on their own, but only in minds, unthinking things are ideas in minds. Some of them are ideas of real things, such as tables, clouds, this book, a shoe, a ship, a shrimp, or an ocean. They are collections of ideas that have been seen to go together [P 1], but their essences nevertheless consist in their being perceived. So, too, for altogether fanciful ideas, such as the unicorn in the garden, the pot of gold at the end of the rainbow, or my jump shot to win the National Basketball Association championship. Both fanciful ideas and real things are ideas in minds.

Berkeley does not mean that my shoes, this book, the Atlantic, or other such objects are unreal. Nor does he mean that every idea of mine, or yours, tells how the world really is. You might wonder how Berkeley can reasonably maintain the distinction between reality and dreams or illusions, or between sensing and hallucinating or imagining. Every sensible person understands there is a difference between my dreaming that I have won the lottery and my actually winning the lottery. If I only dream that I have won, but begin spending the proceeds, I am a fool. Berkeley knew this well enough. Understanding how he makes the distinction is key to understanding Berkeley. We will review the issues in Chapter Three.

Berkeley's Life

George Berkeley (pronounced *BAR-klee*) was born on March 12, 1685, near Kilkenny, about sixty miles southwest of Dublin, of English descent. He went to Kilkenny College when he was eleven years of age and was enrolled at Trinity College, Dublin at the age of fifteen. He graduated with a BA degree in 1704 after studying philosophy, logic, mathematics, and languages. He published two mathematical works in 1707 and was made a Junior Fellow of the College in that same year.

The next six years saw the development of the philosophical ideas for which Berkeley is best known as well as the publication of his major philosophical works. Berkeley kept a kind of journal of his ideas for a little over a year starting in 1707. These were not published in Berkeley's lifetime, but only much later: in 1871, edited by A. C. Fraser, as *Commonplace Book of occasional Metaphysical Thoughts,* and in an edition edited by A. A. Luce in 1944 under the title, *Philosophical Commentaries.* The journals consist of a great volume of short entries, such as:

> Mem. Much to recommend and approve of experimental philosophy. [C 498]
>
> Mind is a congeries of perceptions. Take away Perceptions & you take away the Mind put the Perceptions & you put the mind. [C 580]
>
> Mem. To be eternally banishing metaphysics, &c., and recalling men to Common Sense. [C 751]

In these entries, we see the formation of Berkeley's key ideas and the rejections of various alternatives. By 1709, Berkeley had worked through most of the elements of his philosophy, and in that year he published the first of his major philosophical works, *An Essay towards a New Theory of Vision.* In the *New Theory of Vision,* he criticizes the doctrine of abstract ideas and offers his theory of language, but the work is probably best know for its attack on René Descartes' theory of distance perception. Berkeley argued that distance was neither *perceived* by sight, nor could it be *inferred* from visual information alone, and he held that the objects of sight and touch are, strictly speaking, different things. The book was received cordially, and a second edition followed shortly. Although it does not explicitly mention immaterialism, the journals make it clear that Berkeley was committed to the doctrine already.

Berkeley was ordained as a deacon in the Church of Ireland in 1709, in order to meet statutory requirements of the College. The next year, he was ordained a priest and published what he intended to be his master work: *A Treatise Concerning the Principles of Human Knowledge.* The subtitle amply illustrates Berkeley's aims: *wherein the chief causes of error and difficulty in the sciences, with the grounds of scepticism,*

5

atheism, and irreligion are inquired into. The *Principles,* as the work has come to be known, appeared as Part One. The manuscript Berkeley later wrote for Part Two was destroyed; Berkeley never rewrote it and no part of it was ever published.

This book, indeed all Berkeley's works now regarded as classics of modern philosophy, was poorly received. Berkeley's central claims were regarded as highly counterintuitive, and few important thinkers at the time counted them as worth serious study. Berkeley sought to make them more attractive by reworking the main arguments in dialogue form. *Three Dialogues Between Hylas and Philonous, in opposition to sceptics and atheists* was published in 1713.

Berkeley moved to London that year and never again occupied himself in the work of the College, although he was made Senior Fellow in 1717. In London, he met a number of literary figures and other intellectuals, including Addison, Pope, and Swift. He learned that his *Principles* was widely known, but little read. His ideas were the subject of ridicule. After a couple years in London, Berkeley signed on as chaplain to Lord Peterborough, with whom he toured Europe for two years, meeting Continental thinkers, including Malebranche, whose work Berkeley had long known. After two years back in London, Berkeley lived in Europe, mainly in Italy, for four years, returning at last to Dublin in 1721 to receive the Doctor of Divinity degree.

Berkeley was becoming concerned with economic conditions in Britain and dissatisfied at what he took to be a backward and corrupt outlook throughout Europe. The South Sea Trading Company sold public shares in its anticipated profits from mining and trading operations in the New World. Speculators bid the price of the shares up ferociously, and new companies sprang up rapidly claiming prospects of returns as good or better than anticipated for South Sea. Investors feared missing the opportunity of a lifetime, and practically threw money at anyone with a "New World" business strategy, no matter how implausible. In September, 1720, buyers vanished. The "South Sea Bubble," as it came to be called, burst suddenly, and fortunes and reputations were ruined.

The events left England economically unsettled: investors and businesspeople were rightly uncertain what rules of good conduct were in operation. Berkeley took this as evidence of an immoral preference for private gain over the public good and as evidence of corruption. The next year, Berkeley addressed these issues in his second major political work, *An Essay towards preventing the Ruin of Great Britain.* (His first, *Passive Obedience,* had appeared in 1712.) A work of greater philosophical significance appeared, as well, namely *De motu* ("On Motion"), in which Berkeley offered some of his philosophy of science.

In 1723, Berkeley received a sizable inheritance–one that had once been meant for Swift–and over the next years he began to militate for a project he meant to crown his career and life. Berkeley saw in the New World an opportunity to build something fresh and superior to Britain and Continental Europe. He fixed his mind on establishing a college to educate the children of European settlers, together with African- and Native American youth. He chose Bermuda as the site of his prospective institution, apparently expecting the promise of education and Christian training that it would offer would suffice to lead people to travel great distances to partake of it.

He was made Dean of Derry in 1724 and held the title nominally until he became Bishop of Cloyne in 1734, but Berkeley never actually resided in Derry. Instead, he lobbied for his Bermuda project. A number of prominent people promised financial support, and the House of Commons passed a bill offering twenty thousand pounds for the project. George I gave Berkeley a charter for the college, but the actual funds were slow to come.

Berkeley waited and lobbied. Finally, about six weeks after his marriage to Anne Foster, they set sail on their own initiative, arriving in Newport, Rhode Island after a difficult journey. It was 1729, and Berkeley had every reason to think that he had relinquished a career in the Church. He bought a farm, built a house, and Anne gave birth to their first child, Henry, that summer. Berkeley was the greatest celebrity to visit New England. He corresponded with and met numerous scholars and philosophers, including the American Samuel Johnson, who became first president of what is now Columbia University. During this period he wrote the work which proved most popular in his own day, the dialogues *Alciphron, or the minute philosopher.* Many of the scenes are set in surroundings Berkeley knew in Rhode Island.

By 1731, it was clear that the promised financial support would not be forthcoming. Berkeley finished Alciphron, and Anne gave birth to their second child, Lucia. They decided to return to Britain as soon as mother and child were well, but Lucia died. (Of their seven children together, three died as infants, and one, William, as a teenager.) Four days later, they left for Boston. Berkeley donated his library to Yale College, and the next month George, Anne, and Henry returned to London. They never visited Bermuda.

Alciphron was published, anonymously, in two volumes, in 1732, but Berkeley could not have seriously meant to obscure his identity, since the second volume included the *New Theory of Vision,* which had appeared in his name twenty-three years previously. *Alciphron* was a phenomenon: further editions were published in Dublin and London in 1732, and it was widely discussed–although some of the critical responses veered into abuse. Some viewed the work as only Christian apologetics, or simply as too speculative, but many others took it seriously. Several of Berkeley's more obvious targets in the work responded publicly, David Hume appears to have relied on some part of it in preparing his own *Dialogues on Natural Religion,* and Samuel Johnson relied on it for his *Elementa philosophica*–which he dedicated to Berkeley. The book appeared in Dutch and French translations in the next few years, again in English once before Berkeley's death, and in four British and one American edition bearing his name before 1804.

In *De Motu,* Berkeley had criticized Newton's mathematical conception of force and absolute space as meaningless. In 1734, Berkeley published *The Analyst.* He argued against "infinitesimals," which, if they were real quantities, could not be neglected in calculation as the calculi of both Newton and Leibniz sometimes required. He was also made Bishop of Cloyne. Unlike some of his previous church postings, he took his responsibilities in Cloyne seriously. Having failed to "purify the 'ill-manners and irreligion' of the American colonies" [*Proposal*], he set himself to improving the lot of his parishioners, and he lived in Cloyne until shortly before he died–even declining the more prestigious Bishopric of Clogher when it was offered in 1745.

Berkeley tried to advance the cause of interdenominational harmony and published letters calling for peace between Catholics and Protestants. The poverty he saw led him to reflect on larger causes of wealth and poverty, including personal traits such as indolence and ignorance, but also absentee landholding, the monetary system, and commodity trade relationships. He sought the cooperation of Catholic clergy for bettering the economic lives of the Irish, and he published his economic ideas in three parts as *The Querist* in 1735-37.

While in America, Berkeley had become convinced that "tarwater," a concoction made from the sap of pine tree bark, was a cure for a great variety of serious diseases as well as lesser physical and mental maladies. The virtues of tarwater were the central theme of Berkeley's last few publications. The most notable of these, for it includes also further thoughts on philosophy of science and the history of philosophy, as well as metaphysical speculation, is his *Siris: A Chain of Philosophical Reflexions and Inquiries concerning the virtues of Tarwater, and divers other subjects connected together and arising from one another,* published in 1744. Berkeley seriously believed in the curative properties of tarwater, and his defenses of its virtues reflect the concern for human suffering and well-being for which he was labeled, "the Good Bishop."

In 1752, Berkeley gave up his Bishopric and settled in Oxford, with his wife and their son who was at Christ Church. The third British edition of *Alciphron,* as revised in light of criticism, was published that year. In January of 1753, Berkeley died suddenly, while listening to his wife read aloud from the Bible. He was buried in Christ Church, where his grave and a memorial marker remain. For his "prophecy," in his only known serious poem, heralding America as a dramatic, golden age, a town in California took his name, if not its pronunciation.

Intellectual Context

As, perhaps, the greeting of the philosophical works of 1710 and 1713 suggests, Berkeley was taken to be badly out of step with his time. It is true that his central theses are startling. Nonetheless, in retrospect, they may be seen as very much in tune with the times: Berkeley extends the prevailing empiricist ideas in response to the important philosophical issues of the day. Berkeley was a man of his time but also ahead of his time. Though his thought was not welcomed especially in his day, it has been enormously influential.

In the remainder of this chapter, we trace the intellectual history of those important issues and ideas to provide context for Berkeley's thought. In the next, we turn our attention to explicating Berkeley's own arguments and theories.

René Descartes' "Egocentric Predicament"

To understand the intellectual context of Berkeley's thought, we would do well to review the history of early modern theory of knowledge. If we take René Descartes to be the "Father of Modern Philosophy," we must surely take his "ego-centric predicament" as one of–perhaps the–central concerns of philosophers in the 17th and 18th centuries.

Descartes had maintained that a belief could count as knowledge only if it was "indubitable." By "indubitable," Descartes meant that it was certain: not merely that he was very confident about its truth, but that the claim was somehow incapable of being genuinely doubted. Descartes' aim was to establish a foundation for doing philosophy–including natural philosophy, or science–that would be perfectly secure and that would prevent mistakes such as Ptolemaic astronomy.

To be included in such a foundation, Descartes held, a belief had either to be itself indubitable and certain or else to be deduced from indubitable beliefs by rules that left no room for error. Descartes hoped that he would be able, by these procedures, to establish a basis for belief in the results of the emerging modern science. Moreover, he hoped that the basis he established would ultimately guarantee that belief might be free of error.

Descartes failed in this greater project. Although he is generally regarded as having been successful in establishing his own mental existence by his standards ("I think, therefore I am"), his argument for the existence of a world beyond that of his mind and its contents requires establishing the existence of God, and he does not successfully do that on his own terms. His philosophy founders on the "ego-centric predicament" mentioned previously.

Descartes was, however, very persuasive concerning the importance of the problem of establishing a connection between our perceptions or how things seem to us and the world "outside" our minds, with its shoes, ships, sealing wax, cabbages, and kings. As a result, Descartes bequeathed the predicament to successive generations of thinkers. "How," they asked, one after another, "can we go behind the theater of images or ideas that we experience in our own minds? How can we turn knowledge of our own experience into knowledge of the real world?"

This problem drives much philosophizing for the next two centuries, and Berkeley should be seen as responding in large part to the treatment

10

of it given by Descartes and by Locke. The next section describes the problem in more detail, explains what makes it such a difficult philosophical problem, and sketches the major classes of responses.

Having ideas versus beholding the world

At any moment I have experience, there are ways things seem to me. Right now, I hear some noises that I identify with the air conditioning, and others that I identify with the music I put on a few minutes ago. If I pay close attention, I can make out the hum of fluorescent lights. I feel the cool keys under my fingertips, pressing back against me as I type. I feel my desk chair underneath me, and its scratchy arm against my left elbow. I see a variety of things in different colors and–I just noticed this–mainly more-or-less rectangular shapes: books, notes on paper, the computer monitor, bookcases, the wall, a lamp, and so on.

My having experience like that is no assurance that it *really is* my chair beneath me, or any of the rest. I might have mistaken another sound for the air conditioning hum, someone might have replaced *my* chair without my noticing, and so on. Moreover, as Descartes himself considered, I might be dreaming, or hallucinating. In that case, it would be wrong to say, "I feel my desk chair, hear the air conditioning, and see my copy of the novel, *Empire of the Ants.*"

But I see *something*. I hear *something*. Maybe it is a tape recording of the air conditioning, or maybe I am dreaming that I hear the air conditioning, but there is something I hear that sounds to me like the air conditioning. There is a feeling I have right now, whether it properly can be said to correspond to the arm of my desk chair or not.

As Descartes put it:

> [I]t is this same "I" who sense or who is cognizant of bodily things as if through the senses. For example, I now see a light, I hear a noise. I feel heat. These things are false, since I am asleep. Yet I certainly do seem to see, hear, and feel warmth. This cannot be false. Properly speaking, this is what in me is called "sensing." But this, precisely, is nothing other than thinking. [1]

All mental activity, Descartes says, is some kind of thinking. Sensing a kind of thinking. When I think, I can think only my own thoughts. So, too, whatever I perceive must be an idea of mine. I can perceive only my own ideas.

This is a good place to introduce an important distinction. We may talk about my thoughts or ideas in two importantly different ways. On the one hand, we may speak of my "having ideas" without regard to whether the ideas correspond to anything else that is real. So, the "seeming sound of the air conditioning" and the "seeming image of the book, *Empire of the Ants*" are *ideas* of mine, no matter what. If, in addition, they are accurate, or true ideas, and not merely imaginings, deceptions, hallucinations, or the like, then they are giving me information about the real world, and we may say I am "beholding the world." My *beholding the world* is always also my *having ideas,* because even when an idea gives me information about the world, I can still only perceive my own ideas. The problem here is to find some way to tell what, among all my having of ideas, is also beholding the world.

On Descartes' account, in addition to my own existence as "a thing that thinks," I can also be certain of the contents of my consciousness–of my ideas, including apparent perceptions and any other thoughts I may have. He did not say that I cannot be wrong about whether they portray the way the world is; he was, in fact, deeply motivated by the recognition that we are capable of serious error in how we take the world to be. From a distance, I might mistake a square turret on a castle for a round one. For centuries, scientists mistakenly believed that some bodies naturally move in circles rather than straight lines. Descartes said that I can't be wrong about the "seeming," or about what I sense or think.

> Now, as far as ideas are concerned, if they are considered alone and in their own right, without being referred to something else, they cannot, properly speaking, be false. For whether it is a she-goat or a chimera that I am imagining, it is no less true that I imagine the one than the other. . . . .
> Obviously, if I were to consider these ideas merely as certain modes of my thought, and were not to refer them to anything else, they could hardly give me any subject matter for error. [2]

I cannot be mistaken about the contents of my consciousness–about my ideas–even though I might misjudge myself to be beholding the world when I am not. When I have an experience of "seeing what seems to be a round tower" or of "seeing what seems to be circular motion," I might be wrong about what is really happening in the world but cannot be wrong about how it seems to me. So long as I do not judge how things really are, Descartes says, I cannot be in error. The problem, of course, is that it matters to me how things really are, so, I want a way to make how things seem to me–my ideas–a basis for judging or knowing how things really are in the world apart from me.

Solipsism

Everyone who takes seriously the ego-centric predicament and fails to find a basis for judging or knowing how things are in the world apart from them appears to be committed to solipsism. This is the doctrine that only the solipsist's mind and its contents exist, or can be known to exist. Solipsism is an especially strong form of scepticism, one of the very sorts that Berkeley intended to confront in his *Three Dialogues Between Hylas and Philonous in Opposition to Sceptics and Atheists*. By his own lights, and you probably agree, if Berkeley's philosophy amounts to solipsism, it is a failure. Berkeley is not a solipsist. He must show that something besides the contents of his mind exists and can be known to exist.

Naive Realism

One possible position would be to hold that there are external--that is, mind-independent, material--things, and that we perceive them immediately–without anything intervening. On such a view, everything we perceive would properly be a part of the real world external to us, and the real world would be very much, perhaps exactly, as we perceive it to be.

It may be that you, yourself, believe something like this to be true. It is the position that the character of Hylas adopts at the outset of the Dialogues. Philosophers today call this view, "naive realism." "Naive" here does not mean "silly" or "stupid," but more like "immature" or "unsophisticated." Berkeley will argue, as did both a rationalist such as Descartes and empiricists such as Galileo Gallilei and John Locke, that naive realism is a badly mistaken doctrine. Galileo, for instance, notes that a feather might tickle us if stroked on the tip of the nose, but not in all other places, even though the movement of the feather would be the same. He concludes:

13

this titillation is completely ours and not the feather's, so that if the living, sensing body were removed, nothing would remain of the titillation but an empty name. And I believe that many other qualities, such as taste, odor, color, and so on, often predicated of natural bodies, have a similar and no greater existence than this.[3]

Naive realism is false. We will review Berkeley's explanation why in the next chapter. What are the more sophisticated views that we should entertain seriously? The two main views that will concern us are Berkeley's own idealism or immaterialism and scientific realism, which is a kind of causal and representational theory of perception.

Causal and representational theories of perception

John Locke, like many of his contemporaries, defended a theory of perception that had two parts: a causal part and a representational part. Both parts conflict with naive realism and Berkeley's own views.

According to a causal theory of perception, I can only know firsthand my own sensations or perceptions or ideas, but I can have some secondhand or mediated knowledge of external things because they cause (some of) my sensations or perceptions or ideas. Insofar as I behold the world, it is because my ideas are caused by things in the external world.

Representational theories of perception maintain that in beholding the world ideas represent mind-independent, external bodies. The precise nature of the representation relationship varies from one theory to another. Early modern forms distinguish "primary qualities," such as size and motion, which are said to correspond to real properties of stuff in the world, from "secondary qualities," such as taste and color, which are said to have no similar properties in reality. Locke writes:

> Qualities thus considered in bodies are, first, such as are utterly inseparable from the body in whatever state it is . . . . These I call *original* or *primary qualities* of body, which I think we may observe to produce simple *ideas* in us, namely, solidity, extension, figure, motion or rest, and number. *Secondly,* such *qualities* which in truth are nothing in the objects themselves but powers to produce various sensations in us by their *primary qualities* . . . these I call *secondary qualities.*[4]

14

A causal and representational theory of perception combines the two parts: in beholding the world ideas are caused by and represent mind-independent, external things. These theories give an account of our situation in the ego-centric predicament that implies materialism and denies solipsism.

The mechanical philosophy

Many philosophers and scientists in the 17th and 18th centuries held that the universe was made of "corpuscles," or "atoms": tiny particles much, much too small for us to see. The origins of such corpuscular or atomic theories date back to the ancient philosophers Leucippus and Democritus. In some ways, the assumption of atomism–that everything in the universe is built on or out of some smallest things–is at the heart of 20th century physics, as well. The form defended by Galileo and Locke is a bit more sophisticated than the view that Democritus advanced–but not much. (It is a worthwhile exercise to investigate how much more sophisticated the versions of contemporary scientists are, if at all.)

Mechanism is the doctrine that what is real in the universe may be described in terms of the "mechanical" properties of matter: shape, size, and motion. According to such a view, all genuine explanation of phenomena must be mechanical, that is to say, phenomena are explained by reference to properties of and interactions between and among material bodies. This great hope was inspired by the achievements of the scientific revolution: that we might explain everything by matter in motion if we knew enough about material bodies.

As you can no doubt see, mechanical explanation requires the existence of mind-independent, material substance, and denies the reality of properties that would correspond to the secondary qualities, such as color, taste, or smell. Virtually all the modern proponents of the causal and representational theory of perception also believed in mechanism. Both Descartes and Newton, different as their views may otherwise have been, were concerned to give purely mechanical accounts of gravitational attraction. Descartes tried to do so by postulating "vortices" that whirled unseen so as to draw things down to Earth. Newton worried that his treatment of gravity was really "action at a distance" and, so, not really mechanical. Followers of Newton in the 19th century postulated the existence of a "luminiferous ether" that pervaded all of space and allowed light to flow as a wave, and the search for "gravitons," particles that transmit gravitational force, continues this day (thus far fruitlessly).

Berkeley applies empiricist criteria for knowledge against the mechanist ontology and philosophy of science. He tells his contemporaries that they cannot have both: either the commitment to empiricism or mechanism must go. Berkeley sees empiricism as the more "common sense" doctrine and, so, rejects mechanism and materialism. Understand, though, that if Berkeley is to construct a theory of things without the existence of matter, he will have to find some substitute for what was then the prevailing thinking on how we explain goings on in the real world and how we account for our perception of them.

Scientific Realism

Early in the *Dialogues,* the character of Hylas abandons naive realism for a more sophisticated theory. He advocates the view that beholding the world is having ideas caused by material bodies, but that ideas resemble bodies only in more limited ways, not in every respect. Because of its reliance on quantifiable properties, this sort of view can be called "scientific realism." Berkeley rejects it. Let me first introduce a version of scientific realism that would have been current in Berkeley's day and then sketch a more sophisticated version that might be advocated today.

According to Galileo's and Locke's views, only those perceptions of primary qualities resemble the mind-independent, material bodies that cause them. So, my visual image of a bright light in the sky is supposed to have been caused by the motion of some small particles combined together to make a meteor as they interact with other particles in the Earth's atmosphere and fall towards Earth. The sound of the puppy barking that I hear, or the taste of the cappuccino ice cream, are caused by the motions of small particles in the external world but do not resemble the motions themselves. This account leaves vague just how perceptions of sounds or colors represent their causes.

The more contemporary, turn-of-the-21st-century version of scientific realism addresses that issue. On this version, the representational relationship is not limited, as Locke supposed, although it is rather complex. We are to understand all perceptual qualities as standing for properties in the external world that correspond to primary qualities. Sounds that I hear are caused by motions in the air in relation to my hearing apparatus, and those sounds represent properties such as the amplitude and frequency of the sound waves. Colors that I see represent wave frequencies, as well. Visual perceptions of shape are flattened, two-dimensional renderings–ovals, squarish shapes, and so on–of three dimensional bodies–cylinders, blocks, and the like.

Berkeley's Intended Reconciliation

Berkeley saw that naive realism and scientific realism agreed in part and disagreed in part, and that his own view agreed in part with each.

	We perceive what is real in the world.	We perceive our own ideas.	M a t t e r exists.
Naive realism	Yes.	No.	Yes.
Scientific realism	No.	Yes.	Yes.
Idealism	Yes.	Yes.	No.

He thought that he could bring together common sense and learned thinking. In particular, as regards the philosophical problems we have traced in this chapter, he wanted to square the commonsensical intuition of naive realism that what we experience is real with the educated understanding of scientific realism that what we perceive is ours or in us. Berkeley thought that those views were both wrong where they agreed most and suspected that the stumbling block was the metaphysical doctrine on which each of naive and scientific realism agreed: that matter exists. He set out to supplant belief in matter with his own idealism. His success depends on, first, showing the failure of materialism, and, second, showing that idealism can succeed. The first of those is the focus of the next chapter; the second is the subject of the remainder of the book.

2

Why Matter Does Not Exist

Berkeley's warning

Berkeley cautioned readers of the first edition of the *Principles* that they were likely to misunderstand him.

> I make it my request that the reader suspend his judgment till he has once at least read the whole through, with that degree of attention and thought which the subject-matter shall seem to deserve. For, as there are some passages that, taken by themselves, are very liable (nor could it be remedied) to gross misinterpretation, and to be charged with most absurd consequences, which, nevertheless, upon an entire perusal will appear not to follow from them . . . .
>
> As for the characters of novelty and singularity which some of the following notions may seem to bear, it is, I hope, needless to make any apology on that account. [P Preface]

From the start, he knew that what he had to say was new and different, and that readers might have trouble apprehending his philosophy. To understand Berkeley, you must see that, although he denies that matter exists, he is some kind of *realist;* he believes that there is a real world filled with the usual objects: tables, chairs, pens, pencils, coffee cups, books, houses, ships, sealing wax, cabbages, kingsnakes, and so on. What is so different about Berkeley is that he thinks that the real, unthinking things are themselves *ideas* or *collections of ideas.*

If you insist that "material" means the same thing as "real," or that "in the mind" means the same thing as "not in reality," then of course you are almost sure to mistake Berkeley's views for what they are not.

> Well say you according to this new Doctrine all is but mere Idea . . . . I answer things are as real and exist *in rerum natura* [in the nature of things] as much as ever. . . . . Do but think before you speak. Endeavor rightly to comprehend my meaning and you'll agree with me on this. [C 535]

We would do well, if we wish to understand Berkeley, to get clear about "the nature and abuse of Language" [I 6] and about what it could mean to say there are material bodies we do not perceive or that real things are ideas in minds.

Language and meaning

The entire Introduction to the *Principles* is concerned with the role of language in philosophical reasoning. Misuse of language leads to many errors.

> Unless we take care to clear the first principles of knowledge from the embarrassment and delusion of words, we may make infinite reasonings upon them to no purpose . . . . The farther we go, we shall only lose ourselves the more irrevocably, and be the deeper entangled in difficulties and mistakes. [I 25]

The first problem–the first thing to note about language–is that "abstract general ideas" are empty. We may have a complex idea that abstracts parts of different things and combines them together–a horse with a horn on its head, or a two-headed llama, for example. We may have a general idea that is "the sign . . . of several particular ideas, any one of which it indifferently suggests to the mind," [I 11] as a figure on a men's room door does. What we cannot do, contrary to Locke, is to have a genuine idea of a person, say, without the idea being "of a white, or a black, or a tawny, or a straight, or a crooked, a tall, or a low, or a middle-sized" person. [I 10][1] Although the figure on the rest room stands for men generally, it has a given color, shape and so on. It is a sensible thing that exists in a mind. Anything so vague as an "abstract, general" person, or triangle, with no particular properties, cannot be a creature of the mind and does not really exist.

The second important point about language is to see how terms come to refer to things. To put it as simply as possible: ideas "observed to accompany each other . . . come to be marked by one name, and so to be reputed as one thing." [P 1] Think of this "cluster theory" of terms as the linguistic complement to the metaphysical treatment of things as collections of ideas. Why are those shiny, green-on-the-outside, white-on-the-inside, tart-tasting, juicy, round, stemmed things called "Granny Smith apples?" Because those ideas are found regularly together and have been assigned that name. Similarly for "apple," "pear," "nectarine," "plum," and so on.

Third, note that the signification of these and any other terms is arbitrary. Language is a constructed, not natural, set of signs. Nothing about "apple" resembles the nature of apples. Nothing about "tent," as a collection of marks on paper, in any way requires that it refer to canvas shelters. We could just as easily call a canvas shelter "net" or "six" or "wolf." We project these general terms onto our actual and potential experience when we refer to kinds of things, and we do the same with particular terms.[2]

Finally, suppose that we want to get the most meaning that we can out of experience. You are holding a Granny Smith apple. What does that mean? Part of the meaning of "Granny Smith apple" is "if you bite it, it will crunch and you will experience a tart taste." When we treat not only utterances and written inscriptions, but also experience itself as meaningful, we include potential further experiences as part of the meaning of a given experience of a thing.

Now, consider distance. We have no immediate visual experience of distance. If distance is construed as a geometric ray extending from my eye to an object in space, I would see only the very end of the ray, were I to try to perceive the distance itself. The end of the ray is but a point. If it is really a geometric point, then it has no dimensions, and, so, I would see nothing of the distance. Even if we suppose the end of a ray to be a dot, rather than a point, the dot would be the same no matter the length of the ray (i.e., distance to the object), and, so, I would still not perceive distance. [A 4:8-9]

What *do* we perceive in what is often called experience of distance? Rather than anything immediately perceived, experiencing distance involves learning some relationships among what we experience. If a chair takes up most of my visual field, I can (ordinarily) feel it by extending my arm. On the other hand, if a chair appears small, that probably means I have to walk in order to feel it.

I learn these regularities between various visual presentations of things and the other experiences I might have, and *this* is what constitutes knowledge of distance. [A 4:9-11] Distance is not a meaningless, abstract, general idea. These regularities are significant, or meaningful: seeing the relatively large chair *means that* I would have particular sorts of tactile experiences if I reached out, or kicked, or sat, and that I would have particular sorts of auditory, olfactory, gustatory, and visual experiences in other circumstances. Note, also, that these regularities are arbitrary: nothing about appearing large has any "similitude or necessary connexion" with being within reach.

Compare knowledge of distance with knowledge of material bodies. If we have an idea of "body in general" we must say that we have ideas (in the abstract-general sense) of material substance. So, the question is, can I project the term "matter" appropriately? We have no immediate experience of distance, on Berkeley's account, but yet have knowledge of it. The visual ideas of the chair are arbitrary signs. They are signs of other potential ideas, but they have nothing necessarily to do with those other ideas or experiences. Vision tells us what to expect in experience–"that fire warms us, that food nourishes" and so on. [P 31] On those grounds, vision constitutes a language.[3] Does the concept of "matter" fare better or worse? Is it meaningful, an arbitrary sign for some ideas I might experience? Or is that an illicit term supposed to refer to an abstract, general idea? The concept of matter is even worse than the concept of distance.

There is no material substance

The concept of matter as usually used is illicit. There is no matter in the universe. No material substance, no tiny corpuscles, no atoms exist in reality if they are understood to be something other than ideas in minds. Most readers find it odd, even ironic, that Berkeley held himself to be a champion of common sense, but that is what he meant himself to be. "I side in all things with the Mob," he wrote in his journal. [C 405] To believe something like matter exists, but that we cannot know it, is to be some kind of sceptic. As Philonous says for Berkeley near the close of the *Dialogues:*

> I do not pretend to be a setter-up of *new notions.* My endeavors tend only to unite and place in a clearer light that truth which was before shared between the vulgar and the philosophers–the former being of the opinion that *those things they immediately perceive are the real things* and the latter that *the things immediately perceived are ideas which exist only in the mind*–which two notions put together do in effect constitute the substance of what I advance. [D 3:179]

Do not be put off. The common person and the philosopher can come together in a new metaphysical view. Heed Berkeley's warning. See whether most, and all of the most important parts, of what ordinary people believe true about the world is true without matter.

Against the existence of matter

Berkeley presents his main arguments against the existence of matter in the early paragraphs of the *Principles* and throughout the *Dialogues.* In the Dialogues, the character of Philonous–whose name means "lover of mind"–speaks for Berkeley, and the character of Hylas–whose name means "matter"–serves as Berkeley's foil.

In the Preface to the Dialogues, Berkeley notes that philosophers teach that the "real nature of things" differs from what we sense. It is this doctrine that he means to overturn, for he believes that it gives rise to scepticism, atheism, and paradox. Hylas and Philonous, at the start of the Dialogues, wonder at those who advance skeptical conclusions. Hylas is surprised to hear Philonous agree, for, he says, he had heard that Philonous (Berkeley) denied the existence of matter. Philonous replies:

> What if it should prove, that you, who hold there is [matter], are by virtue of that opinion the greater sceptic, and maintain more paradoxes and repugnancies than I who believe no such thing? [D 1:13]

They agree to admit as true whatever view should prove to be "most agreeable to common sense, and remote from scepticism."

We only perceive our own ideas

We discussed this point in the first chapter: what we perceive are ideas of ours. Hylas, in contrast, first defends the view that you might hold, what we are calling "Naive Realism." Naive Realism, recall, is the view that we directly experience the world of material bodies, and they are pretty much as we perceive them. According to the Naive Realist, in effect, there is no problem of interpreting the ideas we have in order to behold the world: we experience the world directly as it is.

Galileo showed the error in this with his example of the tickling feather, quoted in Chapter One. Berkeley used the following example:

> Again, suppose I perceive by sight the faint and obscure idea of something, which I doubt whether it be a man, or a tree, or a tower, but judge it to be at a distance of about a mile. It is plain I cannot mean, that what I see is a mile off, since that every step I take towards it, the appearance alters, and from being obscure, small, and faint, grows near, large and vigorous. And when I come to the mile's end, that which I saw first is quite lost . . . . [V 44]

When I draw near to the thing, the small, obscure idea of a "maybe man or tree or tower" is no longer in evidence. This is because what I experienced, what were immediately before me, were my ideas. When I draw near, I have entirely new visual images: less faint, more vigorous, and having the appearance of a tower, say, quite decisively. This is because what I perceive are my ideas.

When Berkeley first addresses the matter in the Dialogues, Hylas and Philonous talk about heat. Hylas asserts that heat is a property of external objects and that its quality in the external world varies according to the degree of heat that we might perceive in any particular instance. Nevertheless, he quickly concedes that a fire may produce an intense degree of heat that is perceived as pain and that the pain is not in the fire. The intense (perceived) heat and pain are, Hylas agrees, one simple sensation. As the pain is not in the fire, but rather in the perceiver, so, too, must the intense heat be in the perceiver.

You can illustrate the point without burning yourself. Look at the figure below.

■

Now, look at it again, but cross your eyes.

What changed? The ideas that you perceived changed.

Now, close your eyes, count to ten, and open your eyes.

What changed? The ideas that you perceived changed. Whatever else is true about the figure–whether it multiplied, subtracted, disappeared, or appeared–the ideas you perceived changed. If there is a material book in your hands with blotches of ink, you are not directly experiencing *that*, because *that* did not change. The things we experience seem to be objects outside and independent of us. It does not *seem* as if what you immediately perceive are your own ideas. These examples show it, though: what you perceive are your own ideas.

Sensible qualities are ideas

The qualities that we sense, are all of them ideas, and they do not all resemble properties of their purported causes. So, for example, Hylas tries to limit the conclusion of the argument about where heat exists; he suggests that degrees of heat below the pain threshold might exist without the mind. Philonous gets his assent, though, that "warmth, or a more gentle degree of heat" is a pleasure, and forces the same concession as for painful degrees of heat. The argument is repeated again for cold, and Hylas reconsiders his position, saying that any intermediate degree of warmth exists in bodies without the mind.

Philonous: Those bodies, therefore, upon whose application to
our own, we perceive a moderate degree of heat, must be
concluded to have a moderate degree of heat or warmth in
them: and those, upon whose application we feel a like degree
of cold, must be thought to have cold in them.
Hylas: They must.
Philonous: Can any doctrine be true that leads a man into
absurdity?
Hylas: Without doubt it cannot.
Philonous: Is it not an absurdity to think that the same thing
should be at the same time both cold and warm?
Hylas: It is. [D 1:115-119]

Philonous then proposes a thought experiment. You might think it
through yourself, for you are no doubt familiar enough with the
phenomenon it captures; or you might try it yourself for real. Philonous
suggests putting one hot hand and one cold in the same container of
water. The water will feel warm to the cold hand and cold to the warm
hand. As the two have just agreed, it is absurd (or contradictory) to say
that a thing is both cold and warm at the same time in the same respect,
and doctrines that lead to contradictions or absurdities should be rejected.
Hylas gives in: pain, heat, and cold are only sensations existing in minds.

Hylas urges that there are still other qualities that may be found to
inhere in material substance, but Philonous presses the point for each of
the so-called "secondary qualities." In the case of taste, for example,
roughly the same arguments work as for hot and cold. Sweetness may be
pleasurable, and bitterness may be painful, but, of course, it would be an
error to suppose that the pleasure or pain resided in a mind-independent,
material body. Moreover, depending on the condition of your palate,
something might seem either sweet or bitter.

Phil. . . . . And nothing can be plainer, than that divers persons
perceive different tastes in the same food, since that which
one man delights in, another abhors. And how could this be, if
the taste was something really inherent in the food? [D 1:147]

Hylas must admit that he knows not how. Philonous presses the point for
odors, and the two agree that smells can have no existence outside
perceiving minds. [D 1:149-155]

When the discussion turns to the sense of sound, Hylas moves away from his Naive Realism, and towards the more sophisticated doctrine, Scientific Realism, according to which the secondary qualities are in us only, but are caused by primary qualities–shape, motion, number–which are real (i.e., exist in things as they are, outside us). The sound we perceive, Hylas says, "is a particular kind of sensation," but sound without us is "a vibrative or undulatory motion in the air." [D 1:168]

But motion is not itself aural, as Philonous points out. In a similar vein, science today says that heat is a motion, but motions are not hot or cold. So, if this is to be its position, the best Scientific Realism can assert is the paradoxical view that real sounds are never heard and real heat is never felt. That is not consistent with my experience. It cannot be right.

Hylas and Philonous turn their attention to the case of color. Hylas supposes that this should be the easiest case for him to make, since it seems plain that we see colors on objects. [D 1:186] He suggests that real colors inhere in mind-independent bodies or "corporeal substances."

> Phil. Pray, is your corporeal substance either a sensible quality, or made up of sensible qualities?
> Hyl. What a question is that! Who ever thought it was?
> Phil. My reason for asking was, because in saying 'Each visible object has that color which we see in it,' you make visible objects to be corporeal substances; which implies either that corporeal substances are sensible qualities, or else that there is something beside sensible qualities perceived by sight: but as this point was formerly agreed between us, and is still maintained by you, it is a clear consequence, that your corporeal substance is nothing distinct from sensible qualities.
> [D 1:199]

Hylas hesitates to assent on the basis of this argument alone. Philonous moves forward with a new line of argument. Although the clouds appear colored, they really are not. Moreover, the apparent colors of bodies seem to undergo alteration when viewed with a microscope, or seen through tinted lenses, or by candle light. Looking at the clouds does not change them, though, so as to cause an alteration in their coloration, nor does using a microscope alter the body to be studied with it. So, if the color of a thing can vary without any modification to the thing, we ought to conclude that, as with the clouds, the colors only appear to be in external things, but really are not. [D1 :185-235]

Up to this point in the *Dialogues,* most of the discussion has recapitulated Locke's arguments against the legitimacy of secondary qualities.[4] Berkeley's stunning next move is to turn Locke's very pattern of reasoning–that the ability to attribute incompatible properties to things shows that qualities of that sort are not really properties of material bodies–against Locke's own conclusions supporting Scientific Realism. The same sort of incompatibility and variance obtain for primary qualities as for secondary.

Consider the supposed primary qualities of size and shape. The visible extension of a thing increases as we approach it and decreases as we move away from it. The shape or figure of a thing changes as we examine it from different angles or with the use of a magnifying device. These variations in size and figure being impossible to attribute consistently, it follows, Philonous asserts, that they are not really inherent in objects. [D 1:241-270]

Philonous asks whether "a real motion in any external body [can] be at the same time both very swift and very slow," and Hylas agrees that it cannot. [D 1:271-2] Since motion must be judged relative to time, and since we can only measure time "by the succession of ideas in our minds," it follows that a body might move quickly if we take one mind as a frame of reference and slowly with respect to another.[5] So, motions must not be properties of external bodies.

As for solidity, Berkeley makes two points. First, a thing's feeling relatively hard or soft must depend on the force that one can exert and on the condition of the limb or other body part one uses to test the thing. The wall feels harder when I run into it unexpectedly with my toe than when I lean against it. Second, any resistance–our only indicator of "hardness" or "softness"–that I feel is plainly in me rather than in bodies outside me. When I catch a baseball in the heel of my glove, I feel pressure in my hand, not on the other side of the glove, where the ball is. [D 1:281-285]

Finally, consider the supposed primary quality of number. Even the number of a sensible thing–whether it is one, three, or a thousand–depends on whether we use our minds to count it in meters, feet, or millimeters. [P 12 ff.] If I cross my eyes, or press a finger against my eye socket, I see two things where earlier I saw one. So, number cannot be truly a property of mind-independent things. It, too, exists in minds alone.

For all these properties, it turns out that we can attribute them to supposed bodies in incompatible ways–as different in perceived heat, color, shape, size, and so on, at one time. So, they cannot truly be properties of stable matter in the external world. Matter has none of the properties that are familiar to us. What is matter? What can matter be?

"Matter" is unintelligible

There are two possibilities: either "matter" refers to a mind-independent substance, real in and of itself, but with no properties, or else "matter" is an abstract, general term that refers to no idea in experience nor to anything else in particular. In either case, Berkeley shows, it is an unintelligible, nonsense term. [P16-20, 77-80]

Consider the first possibility. It is manifestly contradictory. How can there be something with no properties? There cannot be. If there were such a thing, we could not have any ideas of it and could not know it. If we were to know it, it would be by experiencing or reasoning to its properties. Since it has no properties, that is an impossibility.

Suppose, though, that matter had a property we do not perceive: the property of supporting the properties we experience. For us to know that, we would need to experience it with some new sense, in which case the property of supporting other properties would be an idea in our minds, hence, not anything mind-independent. [P 79] What could "support" mean in such a use? Not the literal meaning, "as when we say that pillars support a building," [P 16] but we have no basis for assigning it any other meaning, unless it is taken to refer to "body" or "being" in general and in the abstract.

> [W]hen words are used without a meaning, you may put them together as you please, without danger of running into a contradiction. [P 79]

Such a use would be vacuous; it adds nothing to our understanding. Philosophers might as well use the word "matter" to mean "nothing."

For after all, this is what appears to me to be the result of that definition, the parts whereof when I consider with attention, either collectively, or separate from each other, I do not find that there is any kind of effect or impression made on my mind, different from what is excited by the term nothing. [P 80]

When we behold the world, our ideas do not resemble matter in size, solidity, motion, shape, number, color, sound, smell, taste, or feel. The putative concept of a material substance with no properties–neither familiar primary nor secondary qualities nor any unfamiliar ones–is contradictory. The putative concept of matter as "body or extension in general" is an abstract, general concept to which we can assign no meaning. Both concepts are unintelligible.

People talk about matter. They say things are made of it. They think–maybe you used to think–that they sit on it, wear it, live in it, eat it, and drive it to the park, where it keeps the children on swings from falling to the ground or flying into the air. They think that scientists experiment on it and investigate it. Those people are wrong. Now *you* know the truth: we behold the world, but matter does not exist.

What are the prospects for the Causal and Representational Theory of Perception?

The "resemblance" claims of Naive Realism and Scientific Realism are false, since matter does not exist. What are the prospects for the Causal and Representational Theory of Perception more generally construed? Can it still make sense to think of beholding the world as having ideas that are caused by and represent things outside us?

First, as for the representational part: there is nothing to represent. That is the thrust of the argument that "matter" is contradictory or vacuous. In order for us to represent material substance, we would have to use our ideas. But we cannot have ideas of it: by definition material substance is mind-independent and does not consist of ideas, but ideas can only resemble ideas. So, no ideas we have could represent matter. This is true even if matter had some mysterious properties unlike any we now understand. We couldn't represent them with ideas, since only ideas can be like ideas.

Concerning the causal part: matter cannot cause any of our ideas. Only minds are active substances with the power to cause ideas in other minds. Moreover, in any case where we have grounds for holding that one thing causes another we have observed the two things occurring together. My acts of will are associated with the activity of my body and with my uttering various expressive noises so that I can reasonably claim my will to be the cause of that activity and those expressive noises. I have never experienced any supposed material substance, so I am in no position to allege that it is ever associated with any other thing, nor that it ever causes anything, let alone that it causes me or any other being to behold the world.

So, even if people were to insist that matter exists as unintelligible pure being—whatever that would mean—they still cannot claim that your ideas represent it or that it causes them. The Causal and Representational Theory must be rejected.

What does exist?

There two kinds of things we may know: minds and ideas. [P 86] Minds are thinking things. They are *active.* They perceive, will, imagine, reflect, communicate, and so on. Unthinking things—indeed, any object of human knowledge—are ideas or collections of ideas. Ideas are "visibly inactive," inert, or *passive.* [P25] They do nothing on their own, and they cannot exist without an active mind.

Berkeley writes of the two kinds of things in the first two sections of Part I of the *Principles.*

> It is evident to anyone who takes a survey of the objects of human knowledge that they are either ideas actually imprinted on the senses or else such as are perceived by attending to the passions and operations of the mind or, lastly, ideas formed by help of memory and imagination, either compounding, dividing, or barely representing those originally perceived in the aforesaid ways. [P 1]

Ideas can be of several sorts. They may be sensations, such as feeling an iguana's tongue on your finger. They may be perceptions of the mind's own emoting or willing or cogitating, such as noticing your desire or intention or reflecting about whether to turn the page. They may be

30

memories or imaginings, in which case they must be based on ideas of sensation or perception. If you had never felt the tongue of an iguana, you might try to imagine it by recalling the feel of a cat's tongue. In all these operations, your mind would be active, not the ideas.

> But, besides all the endless variety of ideas or objects of knowledge, there is likewise something which knows or perceives them and exercises various operations as willing, imagining, remembering about them. This perceiving, active being is what I call *mind, spirit, soul,* or *myself,* by which words I do not denote any one of my ideas, but a thing entirely distinct from them, in which they exist or, which is the same thing, by which they are perceived–for the existence of an idea consists in its being perceived. [P 2]

Minds and ideas are distinct: my mind is not one of my ideas, nor do any of my ideas imagine, perceive, will, or otherwise act. No ideas even resemble my mind, since they do nothing like thinking or acting.

To put the point another way, minds and ideas have different essences. Something different makes each it what it is.

> Do but leave out the power of willing, thinking, and perceiving ideas, and there remains nothing else wherein the idea can be like a spirit. For by the word 'spirit' we mean only that which thinks, wills, and perceives; this, and this alone, constitutes the signification of that term. If therefore it is impossible that any degree of those powers should be represented in an idea, it is evident that there can be no idea of spirit. [P 138]

Thinking, broadly construed, is what marks the true nature of mind. For minds, existence is *percipere:* perceiving, but also thinking and willing. The being of unthinking things, though, consists in their being perceived.

> Some truths are so near and obvious to the mind that a man need only open his eyes to see them. Such I take this important one to be, namely, that all the choir of heaven and furniture of the earth, in a word, all those bodies which compose the mighty frame of the world, do not have any subsistence without a mind–that their being [*esse*] is to be perceived or known, that consequently so long as they are not

actually perceived by me or do not exist in my mind or that of any other created spirit, they must either have no existence at all or else subsist in the mind of some eternal spirit–it being perfectly unintelligible and involving all the absurdity of abstraction to attribute to any single part of them an existence independent of a spirit. [P 6]

Although we have knowledge of two kinds of things, then, only one may rightly be called a *substance,* that is, something that exists on its own. Ideas depend on minds, so they are not substances. Shoes, ships, dessert topping, floor wax, furniture, and whatever other sensible things may be real, "are nothing else but so many sensible qualities, or combinations of sensible qualities." [D 1:51] As for minds, I do not perceive my mind, though I can reflect on it in ways that make me aware of its acts. I can infer or see it exists from that awareness, as Descartes showed. Moreover, I know what the term means: the active substance on which ideas depend for their existence, which wills and perceives. Although minds are real and substantial, we have no ideas of minds, properly speaking. Instead, Berkeley says, we have *notions* of minds: we know, by reason and reflection, what the term means, to what it refers, and what sort of things minds must be. We have knowledge of minds but not ideas of minds.

So, there are two ways of being, but only one substance. As Berkeley says in his journals, "Existence is *percipi* or *percipere.* The horse is in the stable, the books are in the study as before." [C 429] Do not be misled by the apparent novelty of this view. The horse and books are where you left them, only they exist in a mind or minds. Real things, "the choir of heaven and furniture of the earth," do exist, but as collections of ideas in minds, not as material bodies.

3

Objections and Replies

If a tree falls in the forest . . .

Samuel Johnson kicked a rock to refute Berkeley. It does seem as though it should be that easy, doesn't it? The guy actually *says* that real things exist in minds, just as dreams do. So, shouldn't kicking a rock, feeling it against your toe, seeing and hearing it tumble, shouldn't that be enough to prove that Berkeley is *just wrong?* Of course, Berkeley stubbed his toe, as well as Johnson did. Berkeley knew what Johnson forgot: your experience kicking a rock is itself an assemblage of ideas.

Still, to say that "real things" exist in minds immediately suggests that they are phantasms that might pop into and out of existence according to the whim of the perceiver. On first reading, this doctrine of immaterialism or idealism presents three problems:

1. Unperceived objects. If things exist in my mind, what becomes of them when I don't think of them or perceive them? Does a tree exist, in a forest, before animals walked the earth?

2. Science. If things exist in my mind, how is science possible? Does a tree in a forest obey laws of nature?

3. Subjectivism. If things exist in my mind, then don't I control them? Can't I make the tree in the forest fall or stand or simply disappear, on a lark?

We will treat those challenges in order in this chapter.

Unperceived Objects

You may already have thought of the problem of unperceived objects. Where *do* things go when you're not around? What maintains their existence? The problem turns up in the form of a question you may have encountered before:

> If a tree falls in the forest, and there is no one there to hear it, does it make a sound?

If a tree falls in the forest and really nobody is around to hear then it makes no noise. That's what might bother you about immaterialism or idealism: that it seems to require that unperceived objects do not exist. And it does require that, since sensible objects are ideas, and ideas cannot exist without minds.

We all know to believe that real things exist when we are looking at them, touching them, tasting them, hearing them, or smelling them. But we also believe they persist when we do not sense them. So what happens to them? If real things exist only in minds, then when *we* are not perceiving them, some *other* mind is perceiving them.

> Hylas: Supposing you were annihilated, cannot you conceive it possible, that things perceived by sense may still exist?
>
> Philonous: I can; but then it must be in another mind. When I deny sensible things an existence out of the mind, I do not mean my mind in particular, but all minds. Now it is plain they have an existence exterior to my mind, since I find them by experience to be independent of it. There is therefore some other mind wherein they exist, during the intervals between the times of my perceiving them: as likewise they did before my birth, and would do after my supposed annihilation. And as the same is true with regard to all other finite created

34

spirits, it necessarily follows, there is an omnipresent, eternal
Mind, which knows and comprehends all things, and exhibits
them to our view in such a manner, and according to such
rules as he himself hath ordained, and are by us termed the
laws of nature. [D 3:24-25]

This omniscient, omnipresent, eternal Mind–God–constantly observes all
objects, thereby maintaining their existence even when no finite mind is
around to perceive them. The alternative is that they exist only
intermittently. The problem of unperceived objects leads to a proof of the
existence of God.

Another line of explanation Berkeley used he introduced *verbatim*
in the Dialogues after publishing it in the Principles. He insisted that this
argument alone should suffice to prove his theory. [P 22-24]

But, say you, surely there is nothing easier than for me to
imagine trees, for instance, in a park, or books existing in a
closet, and nobody by to perceive them. I answer, you may so,
there is no difficulty in it. But what is all this, I beseech you,
more than framing in your mind certain ideas which you call
books and *trees,* and at the same time omitting to frame the
idea of any one that may perceive them? But do not you
yourself perceive or think of them all the while? This
therefore is nothing to the purpose; it only shows you have the
power of imagining, or forming ideas in your mind; but it
does not show that you conceive of them existing
unconceived or unthought of; which is a manifest repugnancy.
When we do our utmost to conceive the existence of external
bodies, we are all the while only contemplating our own ideas.
But the mind, taking no notice of itself, is deluded to think it
can and does conceive bodies existing unthought of, or
without the mind, though at the same time they are
apprehended by, or exist in, itself. A little attention will
discover to any one the truth and evidence of what is here
said, and make it unnecessary to insist on any other proofs
against the existence of *material substance.* [P23]

Let us be clear about this paragraph. You may say that you can
easily think of an unperceived object. Try. The object of your thought
when you try is a conception in your mind. Hence, the object of your

thought is in your mind. Now, the conclusion of this is not that the object of your thought is therefore *perceived*, giving the lie to your claim to be able to think of an unperceived object. If this reasoning were meant to demonstrate that the book, or tree, is perceived from the fact that it is conceived, then it would be a poor argument. I *perceive* the paper before me right now, but right now I only *conceive* my high school home room. In perceiving the paper, I behold the world, but in recalling my home room I only have ideas of imagination before my mind.

Rather, this passage challenges you: show that "unperceived object" is meaningful by assigning it an idea. Look within yourself. What you will find on closer inspection of your "idea of an unperceived object" are scenes in which you leave perceivers out of the frame. The empirical evidence of our own supposed ideas of unperceived objects, that is, does not support the claim that there actually are any.

What about your *conception,* does it not show that there *might be* unperceived objects? No. If "unperceived object" is taken to refer to any other supposed idea, it must be understood as another abstract, general idea. So, if the object in question is sensible, it must be in a mind. If the supposed object is not a sensible thing, it is nonsense or nothing. Real things are all sensible. Those things we sense are in our minds. Sensible things exist only in being perceived. So, unperceived objects, strictly speaking, do not exist.

> Hyl. As I was thinking of a tree in a solitary place, where no one was present to see it, methought that was to conceive a tree as existing unperceived or unthought of . . . . But now I plainly see that all I can do is to frame ideas in my own mind. I may indeed conceive in my own thoughts the idea of a tree, or a house, or a mountain, but that is all. And this is far from proving that I can conceive them *existing out of the minds of all Spirits.*
> Phil. You acknowledge then that you cannot possibly conceive how any one corporeal sensible thing should exist otherwise than in a mind?
> Hyl. I do. [D 1:408-410]

Perhaps a doubt nags at you: things happen when we are not around. Think about that tree, falling in the forest. If we went into the forest together, walked right up to a tree that was *just about* to fall, placed a tape recorder nearby, activated it, then left the forest, do you think the tree would make a sound? Would that prove something?

The presence or absence of the tape recorder makes no difference to whether the tree makes a sound, since the tape recorder is no mind able to perceive. Although that seems jarring, it also seems right: if sounds are ideas and exist in perceivers, and there isn't a perceiver there, then there isn't a sound. When we play back the tape, *the sound we hear* is not in the forest at the time of the tree's falling; it is in us wherever we are with the tape recorder at whatever time we play it back.

The only evidence we have in all our experience for believing that there *was* a sound in the forest is that the recorder makes sounds when we play it back. That evidence demonstrates some regularities in experience: that if we manipulate a tape recorder in certain ways, and at a later time manipulate it some other ways, we hear some noises. The noises we hear at the later time are regular as well; they are very much like the noises we might have heard had we witnessed a tree fall in the forest. They are more like those noises the better the tape recorder is, which is part of what we *mean* by "better tape recorder." A good tape recorder will regularly emit tree-falling-in-a-forest sounds in the situation described, but not in a situation when all the trees remain standing on our return to retrieve the recorder.

These and other ideas of real things appear "in a regular train or series," bound by the laws of nature. [P 30] The laws of nature describe regularities such as the sounds trees make falling in the forest when a mind is present to hear (and see), as well as the sounds tape recorders make when left in forests where later trees can be observed to have fallen. Similar descriptions can be given of our relationship to scientific devices for observing very small particles, remote galaxies, or social structures and norms. We never immediately perceive neutrinos, for instance. Instead, we take bubble-chamber photographs or a signal from an underground receptor, say, as *signs* of what we call "the behavior of a quark" or "activity in the interior of the sun" that indicate what else might happen or what we might observe in particular other conditions.

Science

This leads to another important point: rejecting matter is not the same as opposing science. Berkeley does not criticize science wholesale, but, rather, seeks to gain what is of greatest value in it by jettisoning what is superfluous. Berkeley writes repeatedly of his admiration for Newton, and he clearly had studied Newton's works carefully. He emphasizes observation in science, and he is fond of experiment, but also eager to exploit mathematics, so long as theorizing not extend to speculation about unobserved, physical causes.

There are regularities in my experience. If I pay attention, I discover some of them. I thus learn by experience "that such and such ideas are attended with such and such other ideas, in the ordinary course of things." [P 30] Such rules are the laws of nature. The responsibility of the natural philosopher, or scientist, is not to inquire into any hidden causes of ordinary phenomena, as "it is plain philosophers amuse themselves in vain, when they inquire for any natural efficient cause, distinct from a *mind* or *spirit.*" [P107] We *already know* that only minds or spirits may be active, so there is no point in looking for hidden compulsions. Instead, scientists should do what I do when I learn by experience, only they should do it better than I do.

Force

To help illustrate this in context, consider the concept of "force" in natural philosophy or science. Aristotle's theory of projectile motion attributed to different objects different "natural states" of being in motion or at rest, and different characteristic motions, according to whether they were celestial or terrestrial. By the mid-17th century, in part because of the work of Galileo, the Aristotelian theory was under severe strain.

Everyone knew that stopping motions suddenly required effort and that reducing external resistance could extend motion. Idealizing from these commonplace observations, a rudimentary idea of inertia had developed, according to which motion might continue unchanged if all external influences were absent. Even with this idea of inertia, the dominant view in science was that external intervention was required to sustain the motion of bodies such as rolling rocks or cannon shot.

A generation before Berkeley, though, the idea of force was still not clearly defined. Examples using "force" were mainly anthropocentric: they drew on human qualities or behaviors as analogues. In addition, they were in the main concepts of forces as *impulsive* rather than *continuous.* Some authors advanced accounts in which continuous forces were interpreted as limiting cases of periodic, impulsive forces, the frequency of whose periods increased indefinitely. So, for instance, Borelli had written that we might understand gravity by analogy to a force like a quickly tapping, small hammer, and Beeckman wrote of gravity as a force pulling with small jerks.

Newton published his *Mathematical Principles of Natural Philosophy* in 1687, two years after Berkeley's birth. The *Principia,* as it is called (after its Latin title) did two things along these lines to advance the subject of mechanics. First, it distinguished between *mass* and *weight.* The very first definition offered in the *Principia* defined mass (or body–significantly, Newton used the terms interchangeably) as a measure of the quantity of matter. Second, it defined "force"–but not explicitly. In Definition III, Newton defined *vis insita* (the innate force of matter) as a power of resisting changes in state, whether that state be rest or motion in a straight line. He could then consider any acceleration–whether it be a change from a resting state, a change in speed, or movement from the straight line–as evidence for the presence of a force. This gives an implicit definition of "force," and allows treating forces such as gravity as external actions that affect bodies, rather than as properties of bodies themselves.

To speak in the concrete of the effort required to hold up a body or to impede its motion is legitimate, as it is to speak of the accelerated motion that we actually observe when we see a body in free fall. But if science begins–as for Descartes and Newton–with insensible mathematical posits as its basis it need never, and perhaps can never, connect with ideas and experience. Just as we reject talk of imperceptible bodies, we should reject treating forces without reference to ideas. "It would be better then," Berkeley writes, "if [people] would attend only to the sensible effects, putting the occult quality out of view." [M 4]

Scientific talk about observed phenomena–or even hypothetical talk about imaginable phenomena that we might observe–is quite all right. But

39

any attempt to explain using unseen, "occult" forces is unintelligible. We may refer to the literal *measure of the quantity of matter,* or refer to a change in the motion of an object–to a "sensible effect." We ought not to treat the quantity as real beyond its measure or reify something unseen behind the change. Berkeley read and studied Newton's work closely–not only the very difficult *Principia,* but also the *Optics.* He admired Newton greatly. He does not deny the existence of the *phenomenon* of gravity; only the claim of something real beyond what might be experienced.[1]

Newton himself, for what it is worth, writes that inertia "differs nothing from the inactivity of the mass, but in our manner of conceiving it."[2] So, on Newton's own account, "inertial force" is just another way of saying "inactivity of a quantity of matter." In other words, we may speak of forces or of the observed behavior of measurable quantities interchangeably and as might be convenient to the needs of the moment, as Newton himself does with the terms "mass" and "body."

Newton successfully drew together phenomena that had been viewed as disparate–including free fall, projectile motion, planetary motion, and tidal motion–under one general name. [P 104] That kind of formulation of a law of nature is paradigmatic of good science, as Berkeley understands it, and he sees nothing to prevent further such scientific advances. Nor does he think any previous scientific advance need be lost: what others take to be explanation by matter in motion, Berkeley takes to be explanation by identifying an observed regularity in perceived qualities. [P 50] In all this, we may take Newton literally.

Not even all scientific talk about forces as unperceived is completely unacceptable. Mathematical hypotheses about "forces" may be very useful for calculating what other observations we might make.[3] If, on the other hand, a natural philosopher means to attribute the force in question as a physical property of things in the world, that is altogether illegitimate.

Explanation

Some have said, not that Berkeley is anti-science, but rather that he conceives of science as a purely descriptive, rather than explanatory, enterprise.[4] To claim science is just descriptive is to say science restates what we observe, without offering any understanding or insight into how the world works. This is not Berkeley's view of science.

Berkeley asserts that natural philosophers differ from ordinary folk not in knowing different causes of phenomena but in having a "greater largeness of comprehension." [P 105] He obviously thinks science aims at understanding. He denies that scientists should slavishly devote themselves to a mechanical world view in cases where it flies in the face of experience or requires positing intangible and unobservable machines behind what is observed. It is enough to take advantage of mechanisms as they are observed in the world.

> God . . . might, if he were minded to produce a miracle, cause all the motions on the dial-plate of a watch, though nobody had ever made the movements, and put them in it: but yet if he will act agreeably to the rules of mechanism, by him for wise ends established and maintained in the creation, it is necessary that those actions of the watchmaker, whereby he makes the movements and rightly adjusts them, precede the production of the aforesaid motions . . . . [P 62]

We expect the world of experience to conform to the mechanical laws of nature and any others. These laws are regularities that we or others may observe. We seek to use these to find causes of irregularity, as when a watch malfunctions. We use them to deduce phenomena, but not to prove them conclusively ("demonstrate," in the jargon of the day), since our deduction always presumes the uniformity of nature. [P 107] Such a deduction of phenomena:

> gives us a sort of foresight, which enables us to regulate our actions for the benefit of life. And without this we should be eternally at a loss: we could not know how to act any thing that might procure us the least pleasure, or remove the least pain of sense. That food nourishes, sleep refreshes, and fire warms us; that to sow in the seed-time is the way to reap in the harvest, and, in general, that to obtain such or such ends, such or such means are conducive, all this we know, not by discovering any necessary connexion between our ideas, but only by the observation of the settled laws of nature, without which we should be all in uncertainty and confusion, and a grown man no more know how to manage himself in the affairs of life than an infant just born. [P 31]

41

Common folk and natural philosophers both attend to regularities that constitute laws of nature. Infants do not do it well, adults are better at it, but natural philosophers do it far more systematically and with greater comprehension. They can:

> extend our prospect beyond what is present and near to us,
> and enable us to make very probable conjectures touching
> things that may have happened at very great distances of time
> and place, as well as to predict things to come . . . . [P 105]

Berkeley was in fact *pro-science*. He sought only to restrict the scope of science to what is intelligible and to exclude vague or meaningless talk. He did not seek to limit the scope of scientific aims except where natural philosophers might mistake the model or the metaphor for the real.[5] He does not oppose science–only illegitimate science.

Is Berkeley a Subjectivist?

Although Berkeley's view is often called "subjective idealism," in no way should he be thought a subjectivist in the sense of claiming that individual, knowing subjects have control over their own experience. You do not control what you see, hear, taste, smell, or feel. You can will yourself to open your eyes, it is true, but you have precious little control over what you experience once you open them.

> The Trees are in the Park, that is, whether I will or no whether
> I imagine any thing about them or no, let me but go thither
> and open my Eyes by day and I shall not avoid seeing them.
> [C 98. See also P 29]

Moreover, you have no reason to think that you cause your experiences when you behold the world. You never see or otherwise witness yourself producing such experiences. If you experiment by trying to will one thing or another, you will find your abilities are limited. The constant stream of ideas or perceptions that you encounter gives some evidence that something is happening to produce it without you.

Beholding the world

There are two kinds of difference between ideas that are of real things and ideas of imagination–dreams, illusions, hallucinations, and so

42

on. One is a *metaphysical* difference: it tells what makes the the real and the imaginary different. That God causes our perceptions constitutes the difference between reality and illusion.

> The ideas imprinted on the Senses by the Author of nature are called *real things* . . . . [P 33]

We will discuss Berkeley's conception of God in the next chapter. For now, suspend judgement about what God is, and note that this first distinction does not help us to tell the difference between having an idea of a chimera or imaginary creature and beholding the world in genuine perception. This is because:

> our *sensations,* be they never so vivid and distinct are
> nevertheless ideas: that is, they exist in the mind, or are
> perceived by it, as truly as the ideas of its own framing. [P 33]

Besides the metaphysical difference, there is also an *epistemological* difference between ideas of real things and ideas of imagination. Two sorts of things allow us *to tell what is real* and to identify those of our ideas in which we behold the world. First, ideas of real things differ from ideas of imagination in the character of the ideas themselves. Second, they differ in their relationship to other ideas. Experiencing the real world and imagination or dreaming differ both at a moment and over time.

Do sensations seem the same as dreams or other imaginings? Or are they are stronger, more vivid, lively, and distinct? When I only recall something from memory, or when I imagine something, or when I dream, the ideas I have are a kind of copies, and they are more faint, less lively, less vivid. If that is generally true, then the presumption of Descartes' "Dream Argument" is just wrong. The Dream Argument held that, because I sometimes dream vividly, at any given time, no matter what my experience is like, I could be dreaming, even though I think myself awake. When I look around the room now, it seems real and I think I'm awake in my office, but, for all I know I might still be in bed, merely dreaming that I am awake. As a result, Descartes argued, I seem to have no guarantee that I can tell what is the real world and what is illusion.

Descartes, of course, eventually submitted that God, "who is no deceiver," could serve to guarantee the reliability of my most "clear and distinct" perceptions. But we need not rely on any notion of God in holding that we can tell what experiences are show us the real world.

There is something different about how things seem when we are awake, experiencing the real world, than when we sleep and dream, or imagine in any other way, he urges. Dreams may be vivid for their oddness, but otherwise they are pale comparisons of the resplendent, colorful luster of our waking lives. [P 29-34]

Still, does experience of the real world *seem* so different from dreaming or hallucinating? Some dreams are very vivid. Even less vivid dreams sometimes leave sufficiently strong impressions that later the dreamer wonders whether the events of the dream really took place or not. Also, even if we could easily distinguish the two kinds of experience, the difference in how they seem alone does not necessarily reveal to us which is sensation and which is imagination.

Suppose that some of my experiences had a red, white, and green, capital letter "D" in the lower right corner of my visual field–much the way that some television shows identify their network of origin. Would I know that the ones with the "D" were dreams, and the other waking experiences? No. I have to learn which network uses the peacock and which the big eye. It could easily be the other way around and, so, too with dreaming. As Chaung-tzu writes:

> Last night Chuang Chou dreamed he was a butterfly . . . and
> did not know about Chou. When all of a sudden he awoke, he
> was Chou with all his wits about him. He does not know
> whether he is Chou who dreams he is a butterfly or a butterfly
> who dreams he is Chou.[6]

There are two answers to these worries: the difference between sensation and dreaming over time, and the evidence that things exist outside our own minds. Between the two, even if you do not accept that dreaming and experiencing the real world appear different, you should be able to distinguish the two.

Often when I have taught Descartes' *Meditations* in a class, students have objected that his argument does not make sense to them, that their dreams are not like their waking experiences. Sometimes, this means that they agree with Berkeley that the two sorts of experience *appear* different or are *different in character,* even without the big "Dream Network" label. After more discussion, though, it usually proves to be the case that my students mean something else. They mean that they can tell the difference on reflection, because dreams are just crazy: you're running on the golf course with Samuel L. Jackson, then you're in a helicopter with your mother and your friend's older sister, then suddenly you're at a big concert but you can't tell who is on stage, and then you're taking an exam wearing a large cardboard box. Individual scenes make very little sense, and transitions between them are abrupt, to say the least. People appear and disappear suddenly, you cross vast distances in a moment with no means of transport–the things in your dreams do not obey physical laws.

This is precisely the other difference that allows us to tell which ideas are of real things: ideas of real things have orderly, coherent relationships with other ideas of real things over time. Whereas dreams may be all haphazard, sensations happen "in a regular train or series," and are more steady, orderly, and coherent. [P 30] When we behold the world, our ideas are bound to obey the laws of nature. Once we learn some laws of nature through experience, we are in a position to test other ideas experimentally to confirm that they are of real things: if they violate the laws of nature, then the ideas in question are of our own making, not of real things (or else we were wrong about the laws). So, besides the allegation that experience of the real world just seems different from dreaming, there is another way to tell what is real. We identify patterns in our experience of the world and orderly relationships among our ideas of real things. These are the laws of nature. We can test for the legitimacy of new experiences by seeing whether they cohere with that established, lawlike order.

So, although the being of unthinking things is a function of their being perceived, our knowledge of them is due to our ascertaining that particular ideas are more coherent and orderly. The knowledge of that order makes us better able "to regulate our actions for the benefit of life." [P 31] Without being able to learn the laws of nature, we would not know how to conduct ourselves in the world. Learning the laws of nature by experience teaches that "food nourishes, sleep refreshes," and that "the sun I see by day is the real sun, and that which I imagine by night is the idea of the former." [P 31, 36]

Solipsism

Finally, how do I know that those real things are not just in my mind? To answer this question, Berkeley again revives an argument of Locke's. Locke argued that we have good reason to think that solipsism is false and that something must exist outside us to cause our sensations: our sensations are largely out of our own control and are also orderly and coherent. Berkeley and Locke disagree about the nature of the cause of our sensations–whether it is material substance or not–but Berkeley approves of Locke's basic argument.

You might wonder why Berkeley would accept Locke's argument against solipsism without accepting his conclusion that matter exists. There are three reasons:

1. The idea of matter is unintelligible: either contradictory or vacuous.

2. Matter has no properties that we know, nor do we understand how it could produce ideas in a mind.

3. Minds are active. We know that minds can produce and exhibit ideas, which makes them good candidates.

The conclusions of our investigation of matter, recall, were that if matter were to exist, it could have no properties, and that we could know the existence of matter neither by sense nor by reason. So, there should be something else that causes our experience of real, unthinking things.

Even if we were to have a coherent, meaningful concept of matter, mind is a better candidate to cause ideas of real things than matter. Minds are active. We know that minds can produce and exhibit ideas. We know nothing of the sort about matter or anything else.

> That a being endowed with knowledge and will, should produce or exhibit ideas, is easily understood. But that a being which is utterly destitute of these faculties should be able to produce ideas, or in any sort to affect an intelligence, this I can never understand. [D 3:91]

I am exhibiting and producing ideas right now, across space and time, from my black chair with wheels on the bottom. Did you think of a chair? Did you think of wheels? That was *my mind* causing ideas in *yours*. I *exhibited* some ideas, with a lot of help from an editor, a publisher, and, I hope, a bookseller. I *produced* some ideas in your mind. This is an utterly familiar phenomenon; we experience it daily. Minds not only have ideas within themselves, they exhibit ideas as well. Minds produce or bring about ideas in other minds. Minds are not only active in imagining and reflecting; they sometimes cause ideas in other minds.

Matter is a bad choice, for a number of reasons, and we know minds can produce ideas, so it makes sense to think that a mind is the cause of our ideas of real things. This analysis of how ideas are produced in our minds is Berkeley's answer to the mind-body problem. Descartes, having divided the world into thinking, willing, mental substance, and spatial, inactive, material substance, was left with the problem of how to explain their apparent interaction. If mind and matter have nothing in common, how can actions in the world of matter produce ideas in my mind, and how can my will produce effects in the material world?

Descartes never had a satisfactory answer. Berkeley avoids the problem by treating the interaction as mental, rather than mental and material. That reduces the problem to the more familiar phenomenon of communication. He had this idea in his youth, but did not formulate the argument until his stay in the New World. Once he did, he used it to provide yet another argument for the existence of God. We will review that argument in the next chapter.

4
God

God's Role

Among all minds one is special: the mind that is God. In Berkeley's philosophy, God is the ground of being: he sustains the existence of unthinking things by perceiving them (at least) when no finite mind does so. God is also the "Author of nature" who brings real things into existence, by causing them to exist in our minds.

Some people are averse to Berkeley's theories because of the central role they assign to God. Berkeley himself knew this might be a problem. He took the position that his view is no more odd and probably less odd than basing all on unknowable matter.[1] Whether one takes matter, or finite minds, or God as fundamental, one must beg the same amount of existence, in William James' phrase.[2] This is not to say that relying on God in this manner is entirely unproblematic, only to note that objecting merely on the basis of his invocation of God is premature.

One issue surrounding supposed proofs for the existence of God is whether they prove "the right God." It is sometimes said of Anselm's Ontological Argument, for instance, that even if it were sound it would fail. This is because, in the Christian tradition in which Anselm worked, God is supposed to be omnipotent, omniscient, and benevolent, while the Ontological Argument does not prove those properties for God.

The God in Berkeley's proofs is a good nominee. This being:

- maintains the existence of real things when no finite mind is around to perceive them, and

- causes all the perceptions of everyone whenever they behold the world.

What a powerful being! This God would be omniscient, or all-knowing, since it would have everything in its mind. This God would be omnipotent, or all-powerful, since it would make real events.

The other quality usually attributed to God in the Western tradition is benevolence. Is the God Berkeley describes benevolent? Yes: the orderliness of our ideas of real things "sufficiently testifies to the wisdom and benevolence of its author." [P 30] Moreover, the orderliness of experience testifies further to God's benevolence because it allows us to learn and to choose actions that will bring pleasure and alleviate pain.

Berkeley's Three Arguments for God

Sustainer of real, unthinking things

The argument is made succinctly in the Dialogues:

> Hylas: Supposing you were annihilated, cannot you conceive it possible, that things perceived by sense may still exist?
> Philonous: I can; but then it must be in another mind. When I deny sensible things an existence out of the mind, I do not mean my mind in particular, but all minds. Now it is plain they have an existence exterior to my mind, since I find them by experience to be independent of it. There is therefore some other mind wherein they exist, during the intervals between the times of my perceiving them: as likewise they did before

my birth, and would do after my supposed annihilation. And as the same is true with regard to all other finite created spirits, it necessarily follows, there is an omnipresent, eternal Mind, which knows and comprehends all things, and exhibits them to our view in such a manner, and according to such rules as he himself hath ordained, and are by us termed the laws of nature. [D 3:24-25]

The structure of the argument is clear, and it indicates several points that we treated in the preceding chapter:

1. Things exist outside my mind. (since they are independent of it)

2. So, things must exist in another mind. (since things only exist in minds)

3. Likewise for all other minds like mine. (by generalization)

4. Therefore, there is some other sort of mind, omnipresent (for when we all leave the room and so on) and eternal (for before or after the existence of each of us).

Moreover, this mind *exhibits* real things to us according to the *laws of nature.*

This elegant argument uses only weak premises that all Berkeley's contemporaries and all of us should grant. It is not clear what we should deny, if we were to want to block the inference to God's existence: that we immediately perceive our own ideas, that some of what we perceive is real, or that the real things we perceive exist even when we are not experiencing them.

Cause of ideas of real things

Berkeley says God *exhibits* real things to us. Berkeley's second argument for God means to show that God causes those ideas of ours that are of real things.

1. I have a great degree of control over my thoughts and imaginings.

2. When I open my eyes in daylight, I have no choice whether I see, nor can I determine what objects I see.

3. Similarly for each of my other senses.

4. Therefore, unlike ideas of imagination, ideas of sensation are not "creatures of my will."

5. Therefore, some other will of spirit must cause or create them.

6. Similarly for every other finite being.

7. Anything that could cause the ideas of sensation in finite beings would be worthy of being called a god. [P29 ff.]

The metaphysical difference between ideas of imagination and our ideas of real things is that God exhibits real things to us. God is the cause of our beholding the world. As Berkeley puts it:

> The ideas imprinted on the sense by the author of nature are called real things . . . . The ideas of sense . . . . are also less dependent on the spirit, or thinking substance which perceives them, in that they are excited by the will of another and more powerful spirit . . . . [P 33]

God *imprints* ideas on our senses when we behold the world. Berkeley supposes, like Locke, that something other than himself must cause his ideas of real things: solipsism is false. This is an argument that God exists, since matter has been discredited as a potential cause.

The analogy with other finite minds

In discussing language and meaning, I wrote about the projection that we do routinely in identifying things in our surroundings. I do it when I reach for my coffee cup, expecting that it contains the coffee I poured earlier, when I turn left outside the building, expecting that my car is where I parked it, and when I call students by name.

When I evaluate my students' work and assign them grades, I engage in a special kind of projection: I project the existence of other minds. Berkeley writes, in *Alciphron* (Euphranor speaks for Berkeley, as he interrogates Alciphron):

> Euph. I . . . ask whether you admit that there is a principle of thought and action, and whether it be perceivable by sense.
> Alc. I grant that there is such a principle, and that it is not the object of sense itself, but inferred from appearances which are perceived by sense.

Euph. If I understand you rightly, from animal functions and
motions you infer the existence of animal spirits, and from
reasonable acts you infer the existence of a reasonable soul. Is
it not so?

Alc. It is.

Euph. It should seem, therefore, that the being of things
imperceptible to sense may be collected from effects and
signs, or sensible tokens. [A 4:4]

Note three things. First, the passage rehearses a standard argument
for the existence of other minds. We do not directly experience other
minds; we can only infer the existence of other minds from the behavior
of other bodies that we take to be like ours. Second, the passage grants
that we can infer the existence of imperceptible things from what is
sensible. Does that make way for the doctrine of material substance?

It does not, because, third, it refers not merely to the behavior or
motion of things, but to "effects and signs." Euphranor goes on in the
dialogue quoted to offer an argument for God's existence: since we infer
a mind from relatively modest bodily motions, we should infer a great
mind from the far greater motions to be found in the natural world.
Alciphron dodges this version of the Argument from Design by recasting
his solution to the problem of other minds, saying, "I have found nothing
so much convinces me of the existence of another person as his speaking
to me," [A 4:6] and:

What I mean is not the sound of speech merely as such, but
the arbitrary use of sensible signs, which have no similitude or
necessary connexion with the things signified; so as by the
apposite management of them to suggest and exhibit to my
mind an endless variety of things, differing in nature, time,
and place; thereby informing me, entertaining me, and
directing me how to act, not only with regard to things near
and present, but also with regard to things distant and future.
[A 4:7]

Euphranor and Alciphron agree that it is not merely bodily behavior
that convinces us of the intelligence or mentality of others. Facility in the
use of language–arbitrary but meaningful signs–is the surest evidence for
the existence of other minds. This is a point generally agreed to by
thinkers as diverse as Hobbes, Descartes, Locke, and Alan Turing.[3]

Recall, now, that Berkeley argued that vision is a language.[4] Vision is a set of signs–seeing the fire means, in part, "will burn you if you put your hand in it," and seeing a small, blurry person-shape means, in part, "will require many steps to shake hands." The signs have no necessary connection with their meanings; they are arbitrary, since appearing small, say, need have nothing to do with being out of reach. If vision is a language, whose language is it? Languages are *constructed* sets of arbitrary signs. I have not the power over my own experience to have constructed this set of arbitrary signs. So, who did? This is Berkeley's third argument for the existence of God:

1. Vision is a constructed set of arbitrary signs, constituting a language. (From the New Theory of Vision)

2. Facility in the use of language shows the existence of another mind. (From the Argument for Other Minds)

3. So, our visual experience shows the existence of another mind. (From 1 and 2)

4. I lack the power to have constructed this language.

5. Similarly for other finite minds. (By generalization)

6. Therefore there is some greater mind that communicates with us about the order of nature and future events.

Here, in a work late in his life, Berkeley connects one of his earliest philosophical ideas–that vision is a language–with the whole of his philosophy. If Berkeley is right that vision is a language, then, to block the inference to the existence of God, one must either reject 4, which opens the door again to solipsism, or reject 2, reintroducing the problem of other minds. Berkeley offers an argument for the existence of God apart from his unperceived–objects and cause of experience arguments–that is parallel to the standard argument for the existence of other (human) minds. You must accept or reject God and other human minds together.

What is the God who exists? A personal, omnipotent, omnipresent, benevolent God. That talk throughout of how God exhibits ideas to us or imprints them on us is not a metaphor! Vision is God's language for communicating with us; with it he "explains himself, admonishes, and instructs." [A 4:12] If you believe that you have family, friends, and neighbors, then you must believe in a god, for God speaks to you just as any of your family, friends, or neighbors might do. Even more persuasive, God's communication is not restricted to a holy book or day of the week, but constant and everywhere that you behold the world visually. God is communicating with you as you read this book, as you put it down, and as you go about daily life.

5

Problems

We turn our attention now to discussing objects and minds and the serious issues surrounding them in Berkeley's thought. The Berkeley enthusiast might regard these as merely areas for further research. Less charitably, they are the bitter pills to be swallowed if one wishes to gain whatever other advantages Berkeley's position might offer. Alternatively, they might be thought serious impediments to the success of Berkeley's philosophical program to reconcile common sense and learned thinking. For each, I will try to indicate how Berkeley did or could plausibly respond and discuss avenues to or relationships with more recent philosophers or philosophical movements. Understanding Berkeley's situation with regard to these problems provides a useful lens for focusing on important elements of the subsequent history of philosophy.

Objects

Concerning the identity of unthinking things, consider two closely related problems: accounting for the identity or persistence of a thing over time, and explaining which ideas are ultimately to be identified with real things. Both problems are complicated by Berkeley's insistence that the sensory modalities are distinct. The second problem is further complicated by the special role Berkeley assigns to God as both sustainer of real things and primary cause of our ideas of them. In this section, we elucidate the two problems, recount what Berkeley says about them, and offer tentative suggestions about how (or how else) they might be resolved.

Sensory modalities

William Molyneux, whose wife was blind, had put the question to Locke whether a person born blind but made to see could distinguish between a cube and a sphere relying only on vision and without touching them. Locke discusses the matter–which came to be called "Molyneux' Problem"–in his *Essay*, as does Berkeley in the *New Theory of Vision*. Both agree that the answer is, "No." Berkeley goes so far as to insist that visual and tactile ideas have no necessary connection with one another. Philonous addresses the point and takes the occasion to restate Berkeley's theory of terms:

> Phil. Strictly speaking, Hylas, we do not see the same object that we feel; neither is the same object perceived by the microscope which was by the naked eye. But in case every variation was thought sufficient to constitute a new kind or individual, the endless number or confusion of names would render language impracticable. Therefore, to avoid this as well as other inconveniences which are obvious upon a little thought, men combine together several ideas, apprehended by various senses, or by the same sense at different times, or in different circumstances, but observed, however, to have some connection in nature, either with respect to coexistence or succession; all which they refer to one name and consider as one thing. [D 3, 101]

In 1728, an English surgeon named William Cheselden restored vision to a thirteen-year-old boy, blind from infancy because of cataracts. As Berkeley had predicted, the boy, though otherwise at least perfectly ordinary and on some accounts bright, had tremendous difficulties making sense of his visual experience. He had to *learn* to associate visual and tactile experience. He had at first no sense of distance in the visual realm. Two-dimensional paintings confused him.[1]

The psychologist Oliver Sacks describes a recent case in some detail in his essay, "To See and Not See." The man he calls "Virgil" had poor vision as a small child. He fell severely ill when he was three and was in a coma for two weeks. As he recovered, it became clear his retinas were damaged. By the age of six, cataracts were developing, and he was soon blind. He had the cataracts removed when he was fifty, and he laughed, unable to make sense of the jumble of light and color that presented itself. It took some time for him to realize it was the face of his physician.

Virgil had difficulty identifying objects: he said that "everything ran together" when he saw packages on grocery store shelves.[2] He could not distinguish his black-and-white cat from his black-and-white dog without touching them.[3] He could recognize individual letters, having learned them by touch at a school for the blind, but had trouble putting them together to form words, just as he had trouble seeing a trunk, branches, and leaves as a unified tree.[4] And, as with Cheselden's patient, he could not recognize shapes visually, even though he could distinguish them by touch.[5] He worked at the "Y," and was startled by the bodies that he had known previously by touch; closing his eyes when he gave a massage provided some comfort.[6]

The oar

All this makes perfect sense: if the sensory modalities are distinct, we do not touch and see the same things. These case studies support that conclusion. Which raises the question: Should we give up the common sense idea that when I row a boat the oar I see and the oar I feel are the same? Hylas asks:

> Hyl. Since, according to you, men judge the reality of things by their senses, how can a man be mistaken in thinking . . . an oar with one end in the water crooked?
> Phil. He is not mistaken with regard to the ideas he actually perceives, but in the inferences he makes from his present perceptions. Thus, in the case of the oar, what he immediately perceives by sight is certainly crooked, and so far he is in the

right. But if he then concludes that upon taking the oar out of the water he shall perceive the same crookedness, or that it would affect his touch as crooked things are accustomed to do, in that he is mistaken. [D 3:54-5]

According to this theory of language, "oar" is just a term we apply to sensations that "have been found to go together." My experience, though, does not seem like a collection of sensations that happen to go together. My experience seems to be of an *object* that I call "oar."

How do we reconcile how my experience seems with what reason tells me? What can Berkeley say? There are three possibilities. First, there is the "nominalist" view that there is no oar, really; "oar" is *nothing more than a name.* That view is badly opposed to common sense, which counts against attributing it to Berkeley, of all people. Second, there is a "constructivist" approach: the real oar is one constructed from discrete ideas by active minds. That is a bit anachronistic, though, since Berkeley would not likely have thought of it until after Kant.

Berkeley offers another, "linguistic," response in the Dialogues: that whether we see the same oar depends on what "same" means.

> Phil. If the term *same* be taken in the vulgar meaning, it is certain (and not at all repugnant to the principles I maintain) that different persons may perceive the same thing, or the same thing or idea exist in different minds. Words are of arbitrary imposition; and since men are accustomed to apply the word *same* where no distinction or variety is perceived, and I do not pretend to alter their perceptions, it follows that, as men have said before, *several saw the same thing,* so they may upon like occasions, still continue to use the same phrase without any deviation either from propriety of language or the truth of things. But if the term *same* is used in the meaning of philosophers who pretend to an abstracted notion of identity, then, according to their sundry definitions of this notion (for it is not yet agreed in what that philosophic identity consists), it may or may not be possible for various persons to perceive the same thing. [D 3:109]

The word "same" is arbitrary in its signification, just as "oar" is. Whether the crooked oar I see is the straight oar I feel, and whether you and I see

58

the same oar, are matters that depend on the theory of identity built into a meaning for "same." In the common way of speaking, they are the same. But philosophical uses of identity talk might give very different answers. This should apply both to the issue of enduring identity–whether my coffee cup now is the same as the one I poured coffee into–and identity at a moment–whether the crooked oar I see is the same as the straight one I felt. Moreover, this is true quite apart from any quibbles about idealism:

> Take this further reflection with you, that whether matter be allowed to exist or not, the case is exactly the same as to the point in hand. For the materialists themselves acknowledge what we immediately perceive by our senses to be our own ideas. Your difficulty, therefore, that no two see the same thing makes equally against the materialists and me. [D 3:109]

Whatever else you believe, you face the same problems about identity and the same choices to resolve them.[7] We ought to be careful that we are clear and are not embarrassed or deluded by language.

God's ideas and ours

There is another unresolved question about identity, since our ideas of real things are supposed to be caused by God. Why should we not regard God's ideas as the real ones?

There are two approaches to answering this question. First, suppose that real objects are bundles of ideas. Whether they persist through time or exist intermittently, we may think of the "total object" as the amalgam of all ideas of it, for all sensory modalities, at all moments in time. In that case, although each finite mind perceives only a proper part of the total object when beholding it, the mind of God might contain the total object in all its spatio-temporal aspects.

One might object that this belies Berkeley's claim that we perceive real things, but here, again, the matter is the same for Berkeley's philosophy as for many another, including materialism. I am looking at my computer monitor. Do I perceive the real monitor? Where are its sides? Where is its back? Fine, I'll get up and look around it. But then where has the screen gone? And where have the innards been all the while? A moment's reflection should show that, on most typical accounts, we only perceive parts of things when we behold the world. So, this is no objection to Berkeley's philosophy.

The second approach holds that God's mind contains "archetypes" or "models" of our ideas of real things. [D 3:110-113] The archetypes would, of course, differ from our own ideas of sense, because they are not the result of acts of sensation.

It might at first seem that this reply merely restates the problem–why should we not count God's ideas as the real ones–rather than offer any resolution. To the contrary, though, in emphasizing how those ideas must differ from ideas in finite minds, it opens the way to working out some answer, so long as "real" can refer to our ideas in beholding the world. The existence of some other ideas is no bar to that: your having some ideas of real things in no way "uses up" the measure of reality in the world so as to deny me my share. That is so whether you and I experience the same things or not. The fact that you and I have never perceived the left foot of George Berkeley does not prevent our beholding our own feet or other things. So, too, the existence of some real things in the mind of God does not imply that the ideas in my own mind are unreal or otherwise diminished.

These are problems about identity but not a refutation. Berkeley left some issues unresolved, and they are issues that philosophers have wrestled with since his time and work on still today.

Minds

The concept of mind is a fundamental one, but Berkeley has little to say about what minds are and how we know them. His journals suggest that his views changed over time, and some of the opinions he advanced in his published works are at variance with the earliest private entries. In this section, we will try to explain Berkeley's view of minds and some unresolved problems about both finite minds and God.

Identity of minds

About the relationship between minds and ideas, there are three possibilities:

1. a dualism in which the mind and its contents have equal status as substances,

2. only the mind is a substance; ideas depend entirely on minds, or

3. ontological priority is given to ideas, and minds depend for their existence on ideas.

The first is the one it would be most natural for Berkeley to have inherited from Descartes and Locke. That would raise the possibility of ideas existing independently, though, which would be contrary to the rest of Berkeley's philosophical program. Berkeley appears to have settled on the second option in his major works of 1709-1713, but earlier–in the journals–he was quite assured that something like the third was correct. The two possible relations have very different consequences for the identity of the mind or self or soul.

If the ideas are primary, then minds are "congeries of perceptions." [C 580] "The very existence of Ideas," Berkeley wrote, constitutes the soul. [C 577] This approach has the advantage of making it clear that the mind is not an idea and of indicating how it might be known–through its ideas. When I speak of "my mind," though, I mean to indicate something unified. On the "congeries" account, it is not clear why my mind should be regarded as a single, unified thing, rather than a multiplicity. Nor is it clear that it should be regarded as persisting through time, since (I think) I sometimes sleep without dreaming. Making minds subservient to ideas undercuts the claim that minds are the only active things, and that claim is important to the rejection of material substance. So, the bundle or congeries theory of the mind seems unsatisfactory.

By contrast, recall Berkeley's full formulation of the *esse* doctrine: *esse* is *percipi* or *percipere*. By the time of his major works, he had largely abandoned the congeries doctrine in favor of viewing the mind as substantial. This view of mind as having priority is not without difficulties, either. The doctrine holds that the being of unthinking things depends on their being perceived–by minds–and that the being of minds depends on their perceiving. Berkeley sometimes amends this to include willing. In any event, one of the same problems recurs: if I sleep and neither dream nor will, my mind flickers out of existence.

61

Knowledge of minds

It is not obvious that we could ever have genuine knowledge of minds if genuine knowledge requires having ideas. Without ideas behind it, the term "mind" ought not be considered meaningful. We do not experience minds, since they are not ideas. In order to speak of our having anything like knowledge of the only substances in the universe, then, Berkeley holds instead that we have "notions" of minds, rather than ideas. But if notions are sufficient for knowledge, might we then not have the same kind of "notional knowledge" of material substance or any of a number of allegedly illicit concepts?

It may perhaps be true for some things, but not for matter. Although we do not have ideas of minds, and so do not behold them, the evidence of our having experience, together with a little reasoning about its character, suffices to show our mental existence. We have notions of minds because we know, by reason and reflection, what "mind" means, to what it refers, and what sort of things minds must be. The same cannot be said about matter, whose supposed properties we cannot infer.

Animism

Finally, consider one last time the special role alleged for the mind of God in Berkeley's philosophy. God is supposed to sustain the existence of things before our existence, and after, and while we are not with them now. God is supposed to cause our perceptions of real, unthinking things. God is supposed to speak to us through the language of vision, so as to warn us of danger and lead us to better lives. Berkeley offers three arguments meant to prove the existence of precisely the God that would play this role. Moreover, Berkeley's intention to reconcile science and common sense depends on his getting this part about God right.

None of Berkeley's arguments for God establish that there is one God rather than several. There is no reason why only one God must be involved in sustaining the existence of things when finite minds are not perceiving them, for example. Nor must there be a solitary cause of ideas involved in beholding the world–though some coordination might be required to attain the order and coherence we find in experience.

Even the argument of *Alciphron,* in drawing on the traditional resolution of the problem of other minds, raises sharply the prospect of animism. We take the flexible use of language around us as evidence for the existence of other minds, in the plural, not for the existence of some one mind. So, if we adhere to the analogy Berkeley sets, our ideas of real things could be caused by a number of gods, e.g., one for trees, one for arrows, another for oceans, another for computers, and so on. On such a model, the whole world would be animated by these many minds of little gods, rather than Berkeley's intended single Author of nature.

6

Responses

To this point, the book has focused on explaining and assessing Berkeley's own philosophy, with little indication what became of it after his own time. We noted early on that he has been badly misunderstood, and we hope that this text helps rectify that situation. We also noted that Berkeley was in some ways ahead of his time. This chapter elaborates on how that is so, by articulating some responses to the problems raised in the preceding chapter: philosophical developments rooted in or relevant to Berkeley's thought since.

Empiricism at Its Limits

In some respects, Berkeley should be understood to have sketched the limits of empiricism as a philosophical approach. In this section, we will review how that is so, and discuss how these limits are addressed in two different ways by David Hume and Immanuel Kant.

Although it is common today to regard Newton, for example, as having demonstrated the superiority of empiricism over rationalism by his scientific achievements, that is more than a little misleading. Newton was not an experimentalist, measuring the rate at which objects fell or testing whether the hypothesis of universal gravitation could be disconfirmed. Newton did not arrive at his most significant results as a result of experiment or even observation: he reasoned his way to them.

Berkeley understood that this had to be the case. When he criticized scientists for falsely claiming to have assigned causes of motion with the Newtonian concept of "force," this is one of the points he was making.

> [M]ost consider that force impressed on a movable body is the cause of motion in it. Nevertheless, it results from what has been laid down that they do not assign a known cause of motion, and one distinct from body and motion. It is further clear that force is not a certain and determinate thing, given that men of the greatest powers of mind advance different, and even contrary opinions. . . . . For forces attributed to bodies are as much mathematical hypotheses as attractive forces assigned to the planets and sun. Mathematical entities, however, have no stable essence in nature, but depend on the notion of the definer–hence the same thing can be differently explained. [M 67]

The supposed forces in question are not themselves observed. If we were to treat them as real, this would be another example of being misled by language to believe in the existence of an abstract, general idea. If, on the other hand, we are more careful in our use of language, we will note that "force" is a general term for a wide variety of causes of motions. In characterizing it more exactly for any particular circumstance, we rely on the language of mathematics.

> The truly active causes can be extracted only by meditation and reasoning from the darkness in which they are involved, and thus at all become known. [M 72]

How do we tell whether the mathematics is right? Not by–or, at any rate, not only by–having a look. Rather, we must reason about it. Moreover, our reasoning must make some assumptions. You may remember that Berkeley says that we may discover general laws of nature through observation and, from them, *deduce* but not *demonstrate* other phenomena. This sense of "demonstrate" means "to prove so as to exclude the possibility of denial," that is, to establish conclusively.

> [B]y diligent observation of the phenomena within our view,
> we may discover the general laws of nature and from them
> deduce the other phenomena; I do not say *demonstrate,* for all
> deductions of that kind depend on a supposition that the
> Author of Nature always operates uniformly and in a constant
> observance of those rules we take for principles: which we
> cannot evidently know. [P 107]

Science or observation cannot give us conclusive proof of unobserved things because our inferences about the unobserved always rely on the principle that nature is uniform, whereas we can never know that nature is in fact uniform. So, induction must always be hypothetical.

Hume

This discovery, like Berkeley's findings about abstract, general ideas, finds flower in the work of Hume. This section briefly reviews some points of contact between the thinking of Hume and Berkeley on language, induction hypotheses, unseen forces, the mind, and experience itself.

Like Berkeley, Hume is concerned that philosophers exercise care in their use of language. Just as Berkeley treated terms as conventional shorthand for some amalgam of ideas, Hume holds that a word is meaningless if its origin cannot be traced to some sense impressions. This is precisely the qualm Berkeley had about the use of "force" to refer to something non-mathematical or "matter" to refer to a cause of experience not itself experienced.

Like Berkeley, Hume seeks to have experience serve as a basis for knowledge, but Hume will not be constrained by the dictates of common sense, as Berkeley was. Hume pushes the line of thinking that Berkeley began in order to apply it to inferences from experience and to experience itself.

Hume allows that inferences beyond actual experience–for example, that the sun will rise tomorrow–are based on cause and effect reasoning that is ordinarily thought to be based on experience. He notes that, if we confine our reasoning to matters we have in fact experienced, we may not draw customary inferences, as that the sun will rise tomorrow or that this ball will roll or that this pomegranate will be tart.

Hume does not deny that we routinely make those inferences, he only says that we do so by a process of association, rather than reasoning.

> We have said that all arguments concerning existence are founded on the relation of cause and effect; that our knowledge of that relation is derived entirely from experience; and that all our experimental conclusions proceed upon the supposition, that the future will be conformable to the past. To endeavor, therefore, the proof of this last supposition by probable arguments, or argument regarding existence, must be evidently going in a circle, and taking that for granted, which is the very point in question.[1]

This generalization of Berkeley's qualm about "force" severely undercuts our rationale for drawing inferences on the basis of experience. It not only calls into question inferences about the future, but even judgments at present so far as they go beyond what is immediately presented in sensation. Do I experience the tartness of the pomegranate when I see it, or hold it in my hand? Of course, I do not. On analysis, my experience is thinner than I may have previously presumed; there are elements that I have taken for granted as being part of my immediate experience, just because I have customarily associated them with what I did experience, but that on inspection are not present in the experiences at all.

Hume works similar changes on a wide range of philosophical issues, including two others that were of key importance to Berkeley: causality and the mind. We cannot demonstrate the existence of "causes" by reasoning alone, nor do we ever experience them directly. A person brought into the world with the intelligence of a normal adult would, Hume says, "observe a continual succession of objects, and one event following another," but would not observe "cause" and "effect." Given enough time, the person would observe that some things are always together in experience–letting go of a tree limb and falling to the ground, say, or biting into an apple and hearing a crunch. The person would come to associate the two kinds of things as a matter of habit. Still, the person would never have acquired knowledge of cause and effect either by experiencing them or reasoning about them. Hume concludes that all inferences from experience are like this, "effects of custom, not of reasoning."[2]

About the mind, Hume's application of empiricist principles and Berkeley's instincts about language are even more devastating. Berkeley had early called the mind "a congeries of perceptions," [C 580] but came to see that conception as problematic and argue for something more substantial and permanent. Hume turns the theory of meaningfulness that he developed from Berkeley's very own linguistic apparatus to bear on the general term "mind."

The problems here should be familiar from the discussion of the previous chapter. Do I ever experience a mind–that of another or even my own? I am aware of my own sense perceptions. If my mind is no more than they, then I have some knowledge of it, but I must admit that it is impermanent and always changing. Can I demonstrate its necessity as an enduring thing? I cannot. Indeed, Hume even denies that I have knowledge of acts of will of my own, insisting instead that I only experience acts of association. If this is right, then there is no "mind" or "self" as Berkeley, or for that matter Descartes, conceived of it.

Finally, consider experience. Given the tremendous alterations and modifications I encounter in my experience (if I may still speak of "I" or of "my experience"), what are the grounds for holding that it is experience of objects that persist through time? The idea of "object" is another that might fairly be called abstract and general. I have experiences, yes, but I judge that there are objects based on another hypothesis for which I have no evident basis. I cannot prove deductively that the keyboard I tap now is the one I tapped in writing the previous sentence, nor do I experience the property of "being the same keyboard as I tapped in writing the previous sentence" as I experience anything now. Hume's method has similar consequences for objects as it has for the mind.

These specific "loose ends" in Berkeley's work point the way to components of Hume's philosophy. In working on these, and in several other elements, Hume's work can be seen as developing views stated or hinted at by Berkeley. In particular, he extends the theory of language that Berkeley offered and the criticism of abstract, general ideas. As philosophers today consider empiricism, many take Hume's work as either its fullest and most beautiful expression or as grounds for its summary rejection.

68

Kant

In a similar vein, Kant wrote that Hume woke him from his "dogmatic slumbers." Kant's philosophy is among the most difficult, but also the most important and the most rewarding to master, in all of Western philosophy. Limitations of space preclude trying to offer an account of his thought altogether. Instead, we will try to say just enough first, to show one other approach to extending Berkeley's ideas and tying some of his loose ends, and, second, to encourage you to read and study Kant's own thought further.

Kant said, perhaps immodestly, that he sought to achieve a Copernican Revolution in philosophy. Really, he did, but in reverse. Copernican astronomy displaced humans from the center of things, made the earth go around the sun, and held that nothing was the center of the heavens. Kant puts humans right back in the center of things by making minds even more active than Berkeley ever imagined they could be.

Hume's philosophy raised serious challenges about the role that experience could play in the generation of knowledge. At the same time, the successes of emerging science seemed to suggest that reason alone could not go far; and Hume had proved as much, too, in showing that relations of ideas alone could convey no empirical content. Kant was sufficiently impressed with the new science to try, once more in history, to offer a philosophical basis for scientific investigation in general, and a rational basis for Newtonian mechanics, in particular.

In this new philosophical context, Kant is able to ask:

> whence could experience derive its certainty, if all the rules, according to which it proceeds, were always themselves empirical and therefore contingent.[3]

Even Hume assumed that at least momentary sense impressions were certain. Kant asks what must be the case for us to have the experience that we have. His answer makes the Copernican analogy apt.

> Hitherto it has been assumed that all our knowledge must conform to objects. But all attempts to extend our knowledge of objects by establishing something in regard to them *a priori,* by means of concepts, have, on this assumption, ended in failure. We must therefore make trial whether we may not have more success in the tasks of metaphysics, if we suppose that objects must conform to our knowledge.[4]

69

If the objects of experience must conform to the conditions for our knowing them, then, of course, we can know them. But we already understood that, or we would not be asking ourselves *how it is* that we know them. Kant's move is revolutionary, instead, because it means that there could be things we know about objects of experience by *reasoning about them* rather than as a result of experience. If that is so, then we might know about cause and effect relations into which objects enter, for example, without having to get our knowledge of cause and effect from experience. That would be a great boon, for it would allow us to escape the "going in a circle" about which Hume warned us.

Consider distance, again. Berkeley argued that we do not perceive distance, but only come to know of it through learning laws of nature that relate ideas not only over time but also from different sensory modalities. If we apply Hume's critique to Berkeley's thinking about distance, we must resolve to say that we have only habits or customs of association among those various ideas or sensations and, without begging a question by assuming they will go together in the future as they have gone in the past, we have no basis for saying we have knowledge of distance.

What do we make, then, of claims about distance? When I tell my daughter that her brother is beside her, what can that mean? On Berkeley's account, it means something about what she would have to do in order to touch him: reach out or step. Kant's genius is to note that my claim to my daughter is an *empirical* claim that *already implies* that things are arrayed in space and time. Unless bodies such as mine or those of my children exist in space and time, my claim that they are near one another, or a mile apart, is meaningless. But even Hume granted that such talk was meaningful.

Kant argues that space and time are conditions of experience. For us to experience objects and events, we must experience them as in space and in time. Consequently, everything that we experience has spatial and temporal dimensions. We do not experience space itself, or time itself. Rather, they are rules by which experience comes about.

Similarly for a variety of other properties of objects. Kant held that we never experience "things in themselves" or "noumena"; he agreed with the rest of the learned that what we immediately experience are ideas, or perceptions, or thoughts, or impressions of our own. All we can know by experience, Kant maintained, were these "phenomenal objects."

Knowledge is nonetheless possible because our minds are active in creating and shaping our experience according to determinate laws that guarantee that our experience will be of objects and events and, so, suitable to scientific investigation.

On Kant's account, we have no need of hypotheses concerning objects' enduring or concerning cause and effect in order to assure our empirical knowledge of such phenomena. Instead, he contended, we can know of those qualities of objects by reason alone. If we consider what our experience is like, we can reason to what must be true for it to be possible. Doing so, we will find that objects in our experience must enter into causal relations, must persist through time, and so on. Our own minds constitute the things we experience so as to assure that experience makes empirical knowledge possible.

The summary above barely does Kant justice, if at all, but I hope that it will suffice to make some of the relations to Berkeley clear. Hume showed that there were unresolved problems in the empiricist treatment of identity and causation. Kant offers a means to resolve the problems: he accepts something like Berkeley's idealism as a basic account of experience, then makes the mind more active, and more systematic, than Berkeley had supposed. Kant puts back into objects some of the properties that Berkeley took for minds, but he does so by putting the objects themselves in minds. In doing so, distance, cause, and so on were rendered unproblematic by being made part of what we experience–if not part of things in themselves.

Kant's approach also partially resolves the interpersonal identity problem that Berkeley faced. Since the rules that Kant identifies are conditions of human experience generally, they must hold for all persons. That assures us that at least the most basic elements of experience can be shared. So, my experience of an oar can still be uniquely mine, yours uniquely yours, yet we can know that they have a host of causal and other properties in common.

After Kant

Kant's influence is, of course, felt tremendously throughout the subsequent history of Western philosophy. This section discusses two philosophical genres that owe debts to both Berkeley and Kant.

Idealism

Berkeley was in part motivated by a realist impulse. He sought to maintain the common sense notion that the things we perceive are real things. Scientific Realism differs on that specific point, but it, too, holds that there is something real that our perceptions represent. Kant denied these points in his insistence that what we experience are not things as they really are, and that the phenomenal objects we experience do not represent something else. Empirical knowledge is possible, but is not about anything mind-independent.

What, though, if we had some other access to the mind-independent world? What if, for example, we could escape individual consciousness, or transcend experience to divine truths of pure reason?

Some forms of idealism take precisely that point of departure. Hegel, following Kant, did something like that, as did Bradley and Blanshard. Although meant in part to avoid ostensible defects in subjective idealism using tools provided by Kant, some of the same problems that faced Berkeley's philosophy recur.

Consider, for purposes of illustration, the case of Josiah Royce. Royce likened knowledge to "complete thought." Perceptions were held to be true in virtue of their corresponding to real, but mind-dependent objects. Errors were, according to Royce, "incomplete thoughts," that is, mental acts intended to pick out an object which are not entirely successful. When we judge in error, we have "partial knowledge that is sufficient to give to the judgment its objects, but insufficient to secure to the judgment its accuracy."[5]

In order to account both for the possibility of error and the mind-dependence of objects, Royce postulated the existence of a consciousness greater than ours. Time and all things are, Royce thought, "once for all present . . . to an universal all-inclusive thought."[6]

This doctrine implies that there are two distinct worlds: the world of the Absolute, wherein complete knowledge might be possible, and the finite world of human experience. Finite humans might gain knowledge of more complete things–other minds, themselves, the Absolute–by the interpretation of signs. For instance, by producing an interpretation of my past and my hopes for the future, I might come to know myself.[7]

Interpretation is always social, Royce held. Interpretations among different minds establish "communities" of interpretation, and a community of interpretation, "has a mind of its own–a mind whose psychology is not the same as the psychology of an individual human being."[8] Because social minds have "higher grades of being" than individual minds, they can serve finite individuals in a limited capacity to elevate their knowledge towards the Absolute.[9] In this social application of the idea of interpretation, Royce hoped to bridge the "two worlds" problem, giving finite individuals access to genuine knowledge in the form of true interpretations, even though they can have no direct or complete knowledge of the world of the Absolute.

Royce tries to escape the problem of fragmented, individual knowledge that we discussed in the preceding chapter by introducing a social aspect of experience. Even so, he must strain to connect the world of finite minds with the world of complete minds, just as Berkeley would have to struggle to reconcile Godly and finite ideas.

Pragmatism

Berkeley's philosophy also anticipates American pragmatism. Pragmatism emphasizes practical results. Pragmatism tends towards the sort of view that Berkeley showed made sense for science, but applies it more broadly to theories of all stripes. Pragmatism is radically empiricist, and it favors the sort of scientific or non-demonstrative approach that Berkeley also often employed.

Although Berkeley recognized that the intellect must weigh alternatives and trade-offs–matter, but with no other minds? or other minds with God as permanent cause?–pragmatists respond to some of the problems that issued from Berkeley by adopting a more thoroughly pluralistic outlook than Berkeley. Pragmatism is Berkeley after Kant: minds actively construct experience and may even deliberately choose categorial frames for experience. Consequently, experience, knowledge, and reality itself, must be irreducibly personal and also interpersonally varied.

In Berkeley, sensation by itself is insignificant–the mind must vest ideas with significance by noting their relation to other possible experiences according to laws of nature. Charles Sanders Peirce and William James adopt a very Berkeleyan theory of meaning that includes practical consequences as part of a term's meaning; John Dewey and Clarence Irving Lewis embrace the future-looking notion of reference.

Finally, we should note that the pragmatist rejection of 19th century metaphysics is very much like Berkeley's critique of scientific realism.

The 20th Century and Beyond

Quantum Mechanics

We alluded briefly to Berkeley's anticipation of Einsteinian relativity in the criticism of Newtonian notions of absolute space, time, and motion, above. In this section, we will briefly review the influence of Berkeley on the development and interpretation of quantum mechanics.

Over the first quarter of the 20th century, physicists gradually developed an account of the behavior of very small particles–particles smaller than atoms–according to which they obey fundamentally different natural laws than the laws of classical mechanics that govern the more familiar appearances of everyday life. Max Planck addressed some puzzles about radiation, and the failure of a classical approach to resolve them, by proposing that light can be emitted or absorbed only in multiples of a minimum energy level for a given frequency, rather than continuously. He called this constant a "quantum."

Albert Einstein's explanation of the photoelectric effect, for which he was awarded the Nobel prize, proposed that all light exists in such quanta or bundles. This amounted to a generalization of Planck's idea. Moreover, it fit precisely the known experimental evidence concerning the photoelectric effect. Neils Bohr, in 1913, applied these ideas to atoms themselves. Bohr suggested that atoms exist in discrete quantum states and emit radiation when and only when they move between them.

These theoretical developments increasingly departed from the classical world picture rooted in Newtonian dynamics. They required treating some phenomena as discrete that had been previously considered continuous and treating light as both particle and wave. In addition, these approaches seemed to require using classical theories for some sorts of phenomena only, and using the new, manifestly incompatible, theories for others. Confounding questions arose, including whether subatomic particles should be understood to have definite positions and velocities.

What this has to do with Berkeley is that:

quantum mechanics has revived the old question: Do physical objects have an existence and properties entirely *independent* of the human observer?[10]

This question is raised especially because accounting for measurement is such an important aspect of giving an account of non-classical, quantum phenomena. We never see electrons orbiting a nucleus, for example, but only the output of some measuring device.

The physicists who developed quantum mechanics and philosophical interpretations of it were strongly influenced by Ernst Mach, perhaps the preeminent physicist of his day. He maintained that sense experience must be understood as primary, that mathematical equations should be used to systematize observed phenomena, but that no realistic hypotheses should be proposed to go beyond experience. Scientific laws should summarize actual and possible sense experience. Mach was strongly influenced by Berkeley, though he departed absolutely from him in holding that sensations are, in effect, "just there," rather than being caused by God or anything else external to us.

Perhaps it would have happened anyway, but in part as a result of this influence, many of the major interpretations of quantum mechanics rely on very Berkeleyan notions of the relationship between human observers and physical reality. Every version of the so-called "Copenhagen Interpretation," for example, denies the existence of real properties of quantum objects when they are not observed. Some versions, as for instance one that John Archibald Wheeler has advocated, hold that reality is created by the act of observing quantum phenomena.

These accounts are, of course, not Berkeley's. In particular, they depart from his view in accounting for the cause of ideas of real things, and they mean for observer-dependence to hold only in special, quantum cases, rather than for all the experience of everyday life. Nonetheless, they seek to describe regularities in experience and treat *observations* and *measurements* as of fundamental importance, rather than postulating underlying causes. In all this, they are clearly Berkeleyan in spirit.

Naturalism

One significant 20th century philosophical movement is naturalism. Naturalism is, generally speaking, the doctrine that there are only *natural* things. Naturalism has been especially significant in late-20th century philosophy of mind, philosophy of language, and epistemology. Naturalism is often associated with *materialism,* and so it might appear somewhat paradoxical to claim that Berkeley anticipates this philosophical development. Yet, if we briefly review the intellectual underpinnings of naturalism, Berkeley's affinity for it can be seen.

One of the key tenets of naturalized epistemology, to choose a particular area of naturalist emphasis in philosophy, is the rejection of the possibility of scepticism. This was precisely the standard used in the Dialogues as test of whether Hylas or Philonous was right.

Naturalists hold that we should turn to science to help us develop adequate philosophies. So, a naturalized epistemologist might begin by assuming that the ways in which we gather information or make judgments about beliefs are approximately the right ones, go on to rely on psychological investigation of what our actual practices are, assess how they deviate from some apparently attainable ideal, and prescribe means for improvement.

There is nothing in that approach that a follower of Berkeley would be bound to reject. The link between Berkeley and naturalism is only a surprise if one has swallowed the doctrine that Berkeley is somehow against science. But, as you have seen, that is not the case. Outside epistemology, as well, Berkeley could properly be seen as taking a naturalist stance–so long as "natural" is interpreted appropriately and not understood to beg the question in favor of the existence of mind-independent, material substance.

Coherentism

Traditionally in Western philosophy, knowledge has been regarded as justified, true belief. The basic idea is that knowledge is a good kind of belief: true belief. Not all true beliefs count as knowledge, though, for some might be happy accidents.

As far back as Plato, the distinction was made between true opinion or belief and genuine knowledge. In the *Meno,* Plato's Socrates convinced his opponent that since true opinion is as useful as knowledge, the difference between the two must be that one who knows can "give an account of the reasons why," and, so, has a justification. Socrates uses the metaphor of knowledge being "tied down" to a secure foundation so that it will remain with a person. The conception of knowledge as justified, true belief and the metaphor of knowledge involving a foundation dominate the epistemological agenda until quite recently.

Berkeley is an exception to the dominant tradition in this, as in a number of other things. Berkeley's epistemology can be understood as a preliminary form of *coherentism.* Coherentists generally accept the justified, true belief conception of knowledge, but reject the foundational claims and metaphors.

Coherentism in its contemporary form is a response to a particular philosophical problem. As Keith Lehrer puts it:

> In whatever way a man might attempt to justify his beliefs, whether to himself or to another, he must always appeal to some belief. There is nothing other than one's belief to which one can appeal in the justification of belief. There is no exit from the circle of beliefs.[11]

Severing the circle of belief, for example, by articulating some propositions that are indubitable, is a key move in the development of any foundationalist theory of knowledge. Coherentists, though, offer another metaphor:

> For the coherentist a body of knowledge is a free-floating raft every plan of which helps directly or indirectly to keep all the others in place, and no plank of which would retain its status with no help from the others.[12]

The relevance to Berkeley should be clear. He responds to the egocentric predicament by showing how we can make do with the self and its ideas, with the theater screen and its images. He should be amenable to a theory that explicates the concept of genuine knowledge arising *within* the circle of belief.

Recall, if you will, the distinction Berkeley makes between the cause of our ideas of real objects and the means by which we differentiate them from ideas of imagination. The *metaphysical* difference is that our ideas of real things are caused by God. The epistemological story is, of necessity, somewhat different:

> The ideas of sense are more strong, more lively, and distinct than those of the imagination; they have likewise a steadiness, order, and coherence, and are not excited at random, as those which are the effects of human wills often are, but in a regular train or series . . . . [P 30]

As discussed in Chapter Three, Berkeley went on to identify laws of nature with the regular patterns according to which ideas of real things are produced in us. We know these only because we can perceive their order, coherence, and so on. So, where the *esse* of physical objects is said to be a function of their being perceived, our knowledge of them is due to ascertaining that certain beliefs are more coherent and orderly, that they make us "better able to manage [ourselves] in the affairs of life." [P 31]

Berkeley did not develop his coherence theory of justification more fully, nor did he explicate the concept of "coherence." Nonetheless, the view is worth noting for its historical importance, given Berkeley's influence on Hume, Royce, and others.

Virtual Reality

Finally, consider one concept now in vogue analogous to the world as Berkeley described it: cyberspace. I do not mean to say that Berkeley made up the idea of cyberspace or virtual reality; the dream of leaving one's body behind to live in a world or pure mind is quite old.[13] Rather, modern technology furnishes *illustrations* of an immaterial reality, in the extravagances of Gibson's cyberspace[14] or Stephenson's Metaverse,[15] or simply in "the 'place' where a telephone conversation appears to occur."[16] Thinking of Berkeley's "ideas" as data and of our minds as computers on a network, we have one final analogy for understanding and assessing Berkeley's philosophy: all the world is a cyberspace.

In this model, a finite mind–a computer client, in the model–may have ideas of several sorts, including imagination, reflection, and perception. Ideas may be understood on this model as data–concrete ideas. Ideas of imagination or reflection are produced by the client itself, recalling stored data and performing some operations on it. Ideas of perception are generated by the server. The server (God) is at any given time sending data to a very large number of clients (finite minds). It must have a very fast CPU (or CPU's)! Ideas of perception may be tactile, olfactory, gustatory, auditory, or visual. Berkeley, you will recall, holds these to be different in kind. So, on our computational model we should conceive of these data as being received distinctly, whether *via* virtual "ports" of the client or as entered in a specific field–having a regular position in a structured database.

Perceiving an apple, in this way of thinking, involves receiving from the server data of the general form:

> <cool and smooth, apple-scented, no change, no change, variously red>

which is also understood to "mean" (i.e., can be interpreted by the client as) things such as:

- if hand moves toward mouth then will feel pressure against lips,
- if bite then will taste apple flavor,
- if release grip and look then will see motion downwards

and so on.

Whether the perception counts as knowledge depends on whether the perceptions cohere at a moment and obey laws such as expressed in the if-then statements listed. For them to be perceptions of real things, according to Berkeley, they must be caused by God–i.e., in our analogy, transmitted from the main computer server. Acts of will generate signals that are transmitted to other clients on the network.

We have been describing the system from a design perspective. It is very different from the users' perspective. Return, for a moment, to consider cyberspace. The element of projection of self involved in common uses of networked computers or cyberspace has captured a great deal of attention. As Turkle says:

> . . . for many of us, cyberspace is now part of the routines of everyday life. When we read our electronic mail or send postings to an electronic bulletin board or make an airline reservation over a computer network, we are in cyberspace. In cyberspace, we can talk, exchange ideas, and assume new personae of our own creation. We have the opportunity to build new kinds of communities, virtual communities, in which we participate with people from all over the world, people with whom we converse daily, people with whom we may have fairly intimate relationships but whom we may never physically meet.[17]

Being in cyberspace is doing without bodies, just as Berkeley proposed. People communicate with one another and form strong bonds, and manipulate objects that exist only in that space, all without the intervention of material bodies.

Or do they?

As we explore the analogy, we want to claim only what Berkeley presumably could have, had he known about computer networks. One somewhat serious complication is that, if we think of the network as a collection of physical devices, we risk not properly representing Berkeley's position.

You know that real computer networks *are* physically realized. Cyberspace, some say, is merely an illusion or projection and is nothing like a real, independent place. It requires physical network connections that can be monitored in the physical world. It requires computer servers that can be turned off or taken away. It requires running computer code that in effect governs it, and that code is written and implemented and maintained in the physical world.[18]

So, what does the analogy show? Is it just a bad analogy? Does it show what is wrong with Berkeley's views, or how they fail? You might think so, since we have seen that the very Berkeleyan world of cyberspace requires the existence of a physical world outside the system of cyberspace. To think that would be a mistake.

Even if cyberspace could not or does not exist in the absence of the *physical,* that is not to say that it requires anything *material.* To suppose that the discovery about cyberspace and physical computers harms Berkeley's position at all requires begging the question by, for example, supposing that the existence of computers or keyboards or copper wire or fiber optic cable refutes his claims.

Just as Samuel Johnson's kicking of the rock did not refute Berkeley, neither does this point about the physical realization of the infrastructure of cyberspace. Computers, keyboards, copper wire, fiber optic cable, and any other physical objects on which cyberspace is supposed to depend are themselves ideas, just as shoes, ships, sealing wax, and cabbages are. They obey natural laws. They exist in minds. Virtual worlds may rest on a physical world, but the physical world differs in its laws (and apparent causal priority) rather than in its substance.

Cyberspace is "virtual" because we take the physical to be primary. The ordinary stuff of our daily lives–shoes, sand, this book–rests on atoms, say. If the atoms are primary, then the book and your body are virtual. If we take quantum phenomena to be primary, then the atoms are virtual. Yet, if we take observation to be primary, quantum states are virtual. So, perhaps, it's virtual worlds all the way down. As Berkeley writes:

> In short, if there were external bodies, it is impossible we should ever come to know it; and if there were not, we might have the very same reasons to think there were that we have now. [P 20]

Our experience will not simply tell us what view is right. If you seemed suddenly to float in the air, and a neon sign seemed to appear before you, saying, "This part is real," would you believe it? No such simple sign can settle the issue whether we live in a world of minds and ideas or whether mind-independent external bodies exist. We must reason critically, we must think for ourselves, we must decide whether matter is superfluous and whether minds and ideas can do all Berkeley calls for them to do.

Set aside prejudice. Be clear about the meanings of words. Use your critical faculties to answer the question: Which is the more skeptical, the more dubious possibility, a senseless, inert, world of matter, or a world alive, in which physical objects are ideas in minds?

Notes

Notes To Chapter One

1. Meditation 2.

2. Meditation 3.

3. p. 57.

4. *Essay Concerning Human Understanding,* Chapter VIII, secs. 9-10. Descartes makes the distinction in Meditation Three, Galileo near the quoted passage from *The Assayer,* Hobbes in *Leviathan.*

Notes to Chapter Two

1. This is the idea not only behind much 20th century analytic philosophy, but also behind various critiques of popular images and stereotypes. For example, an important reason to avoid sexist uses of language, such as using "men" to refer to people in general, is that "men" differentially calls to mind men but not women.

2. See the discussion of Hume, below, and Goodman, 1983.

3. Berkeley considered, but rejected, the idea that each of the sensory modalities might constitute a different language on the grounds that the other senses were too vague. They give only signs, he finally maintained, not anything so elaborate as a language. See A 7:12 in the third edition only.

4. *Essay,* Chapter VIII, para. 15 ff.

5. Note the parallel with the Special Theory of Relativity.

Notes to Chapter Three

1. He also offers a very cogent critique of Newton's conception of his own calculus, in *The Analyst.* The central argument is summarized well in Urmson, 1982.

2. Following Def III.

3. Compare the so-called "Semantic View of Theories." van Fraassen, 1980, Giere, 1988.

4. Acton, 1967, e.g.

5. See also, Turbayne, 1970.

6. Chaung-tzu, 1991.

Notes to Chapter Four

1. See, especially, P 50, 107; D 2, 29; D 3, 91 and 169.

2. *James, 1968,* pp. 44-5.

3. Turing, 1950, though not without controversy today.

4. This aspect of Berkeley's philosophy is important on three different counts. One is the argument concerning God, made in the main text. It also worth noting that Berkeley offers, albeit in some rather old-fashioned language, a precursor to a very contemporary pragmatic or behavioral theory of meaning. Berkeley does not confine himself to the cluster theory of terms, but treats practical consequences of different behaviors we might undertake as relevant to the theory of meaning. In addition, in treating experience as linguistic, and because he takes phenomenological perception to constitute the real world of physical

objects, Berkeley anticipates the post-structuralist treatment of all the world as text. Not only post-structuralists take this line, of course. For more analytically inclined philosophies in this vein, see the work of Nelson Goodman, especially *The Structure of Appearance,* or Daniel Dennett's use of the idea of narrative in accounting for the development of selves, in "The Origins of Selves."

Notes to Chapter Five

1. Berkeley discusses the case in his *Theory of Vision Vindicated and Explained.*

2. 119.

3. 121.

4. 123-4.

5. 126 ff.

6. 142-3. Virgil does eventually improve somewhat in some of these abilities, but his health soon fails dramatically.

7. All three of the approaches described would find defenders on the contemporary scene. The first and third resonate with postmodern approaches such as those rooted in the works of Ferdinand Saussure or of Jacques Derrida. Curiously, they also echo in some analytic approaches, such as that of Willard van Orman Quine. For, if "oar" is just a name, it is an open question *for what* it is a name: for an oar entire, or for an assemblage of oar parts. [Quine, 1960] The second alternative is of a piece with a great variety of post-Kantian or neo-Kantian philosophical persuasions. In pragmatism, for example, it finds flower both in a more individualistic form and a more social form, which suggests that even choosing that alternative does not yet settle the issue.

Notes to Chapter Six

1. *Enquiry,* IV, pt. II, para. 6.

2. *Enquiry,* V, pt. 1 para. 3-5.

3. *Critique of Pure Reason,* B 5.

4. *Critique of Pure Reason,* B xvi.

5. Royce, 1885, p. 54.

6. Royce, 1885, p. 68.

7. Royce, 1913, p. 245.

8. Royce, 1913, p. 80.

9. Royce, 1913, p. 218.

10. Holton and Brush, 1973, p. 498.

11. Lehrer, 1974, 187-188.

12. Sosa, 1980, p. 24. The root metaphor is Neurath's "boat," which has been put to use not only within coherentism but also in naturalized epistemology as an illustration of the point that no *a priori* knowledge is possible, hence, there is no "First Philosophy." In that way, naturalizers aim to dissolve the problem of the circle of belief.

13. Wertheim, 1999

14. Gibson, 1994

15. Stephenson, 1992.

16. Sterling, 1992, pp. xi-xii.

17. Turkle, 1995, pp. 10-11.

18. Lessig, 1999.

Bibliography

Acton, H. B. 1967. "Berkeley, George." In Paul Edwards, ed., *The Encyclopedia of Philosophy.* New York: Macmillan.

Armstrong, David M. 1965. "Editor's Introduction." In *Berkeley's Philosophical Writings,* 7-34. New York: Collier Books.

Berkeley, George. 1997. *The Works of George Berkeley, Bishop of Cloyne.* InteLex PastMasters database.

Berman, David. 1993. "Introduction." In *George Berkeley--Alciphron or the minute philosopher in focus,* edited by David Berman, 1-16. New York: Routledge.

BonJour, Laurence. 1985. *The Structure of Empirical Knowledge.* Cambridge, Massachusetts: Harvard University Press.

Bracken, Harry M. 1965. *The Early Reception of Berkeley's Immaterialism, 1710-1733.* Rev. ed. The Hague: Martinus Nijhoff.

Chuang-tzu. 1991. *Chaung-tzu.* A. C. Graham, tr. In John M. Koller
and Patricia Koller, eds., *A Sourcebook in Asian Philosophy.* New
York: Macmillan.

Dennett, Daniel. 1989. "The Origins of Selves." *Cogito,* 163-173.

Descartes, Rene. 1993. *Meditations on First Philosophy.* Donald A.
Cress, tr. Indianapolis: Hackett.

Devitt, Michael, and Kim Sterelny. 1999. *Language and Reality: An
Introduction to the Philosophy of Language.* 2d ed. Cambridge,
Massacusetts: The MIT Press.

Dijksterhuis, E. J. 1986. *The Mechanization of the World Picture:
Pythagoras to Newton.* C. Dikshoorn, tr. Princeton, New Jersey:
Princeton University Press.

Dodd, J. E. 1984. *The ideas of particle physics: an introduction for
scientists.* Cambridge: Cambridge University Press.

Galilei, Galileo. 1989. "The Assayer." A. C. Danto, tr. In Michael R.
Matthews, ed., *The Scientific Background to Modern Philosophy.*
Indianapolis: Hackett.

Gaustad, Edwin S. 1979. *George Berkeley in America.* New Haven:
Yale University Press.

Gibson, William. 1994. "Burning Chrome." In *Burning Chrome.*
Revised ed. New York: Ace.

Giere, Ronald N. 1988. *Explaining Science: A Cognitive Approach.*
Chicago: University of Chicago Press.

Goodman, Nelson. 1977. *The Structure of Appearance.* 3d ed.
Dordrecht: D. Reidel.

----------. 1983. *Fact, Fiction, and Forecast.* 4th ed. Cambridge,
Massachusetts: Harvard University Press.

Holton, Gerald, and Stephen G. Brush. 1973. *Introduction to Concepts
and Theories in Physical Science.* 2d ed. Reading, Massachusetts:
Addison-Wesley.

Hume, David. 1993. *An Enquiry Concerning Human Understanding.*
Eric Steinberg, ed. Indianapolis: Hackett.

James, William. 1968. *Some Problems of Philosophy: A Beginning of
an Introduction to Philosophy.* New York: Greenwood Press.

Kant, Immanuel. 1965. *Critique of Pure Reason.* Norman Kemp Smith,
tr. New York: St. Martin's Press.

Kuklick, Bruce. 1977. *The Rise of American Philosophy: Cambridge,
Massachusetts, 1860-1930.* New Haven: Yale University Press.

Lehrer, Keith. 1974. *Knowledge.* Oxford: Oxford University Press.

Lessig, Lawrence. 1999. *Code: And Other Laws of Cyberspace.* New York: Basic Books.

Martin C. B. and D. M. Armstrong, eds. 1968. *Locke and Berkeley: A Collection of Critical Essays.* Garden City, New York: Anchor.

MacKinnon, Edward M. 1982. *Scientific Explanation and Atomic Physics.* Chicago: University of Chicago Press.

Muehlmann, Robert G. 1992. *Berkeley's Ontology.* Indianapolis: Hackett Publishing.

Pitcher, George. 1977. *Berkeley.* London: Routledge & Kegan Paul.

Quine, Willard van Orman. 1960. *Word and Object.* Cambridge, Massachusetts: The MIT Press.

Royce, Josiah. 1885. "The Possibility of Error." In *The Religious Aspect of Philosophy.* Boston: Houghton Mifflin Company.

----------. 1913. *The Problem of Christianity.* New York: Macmillan.

Sacks, Oliver. 1995. "To See and Not See." In *An Anthropologist on Mars,* 108-152. New York: Vintage Books.

Sosa, Ernest. 1980. "The Raft and the Pyramid: Coherence versus Foundations in the Theory of Knowledge." In Peter French, Theodore Uehling, Jr., and Howard Wettstein, eds., *Midwest Studies in Philosophy,* vol. 5, *Studies in Epistemology.*

Stephenson, Neal. 1992. *Snow Crash.* New York: Bantam.

Sterling, Bruce. 1992. *The Hacker Crackdown: Law and Disorder on the Electronic Frontier.* New York: Bantam.

Thayer, H. S., ed. 1953. *Newton's Philosophy of Nature.* New York: Hafner Press.

----------. 1984. *Meaning and Action: A Critical History of Pragmatism.* 2d ed. Indianapolis: Hackett.

Turbayne, Colin Murray. 1970. *The Myth of Metaphor.* Revised ed. Columbia, South Carolina: University of South Carolina Press.

Turing, A. M. 1950. "Computing Machinery and Intelligence." *Mind.*

Turkle, Sherry. 1995. *Life on the Screen.* New York: Simon and Schuster.

Urmson, J. O. 1982. *Berkeley.* Oxford: Oxford University Press.

van Fraassen, Bas. 1980. *The Scientific Image.* Oxford: Oxford University Press.

Wertheim, Margaret. 1999. *The Pearly Gates of Cyberspace: A History of Space from Dante to the Internet.* New York: W. W. Norton.